BUILDING COALITIONS IN THE HUMAN SERVICES

SAGE HUMAN SERVICES GUIDES, VOLUME 60

SAGE HUMAN SERVICES GUIDES

a series of books edited by ARMAND LAUFFER and CHARLES D. GARVIN. Published in cooperation with the University of Michigan School of Social Work and other organizations.

A **SAGE** HUMAN SERVICES GUIDE **60**

BUILDING COALITIONS IN THE HUMAN SERVICES

Milan J. DLUHY

**with the assistance of
Sanford L. Kravitz**

*Published in cooperation with the University of
Michigan School of Social Work*

SAGE PUBLICATIONS
The International Professional Publishers
Newbury Park   London   New Delhi

For information address:

SAGE Publications, Inc.
2111 West Hillcrest Drive
Newbury Park, California 91320

SAGE Publications Ltd.
28 Banner Street
London EC1Y 8QE
England

SAGE Publications India Pvt. Ltd.
M-32 Market
Greater Kailash I
New Delhi 110 048 India

Printed in the United States of America

Library of Congress Cataloging-in-Publication Data

Dluhy, Milan J., 1942-
    Building coalitions in the human services / by Milan J. Dluhy with
the assistance of Sanford L. Kravitz.
        p.   cm. — (Sage human services guides ; v. 60)
    Includes bibliographical references (p.).
    ISBN 0-8039-2604-9
    1. Public welfare—United States.   2. Social service—United
States—Citizen participation.   3. Coalition (Social sciences)
I. Kravitz, Sanford L.   II. Title.   III. Series.
HV95.D59   1990
361.8'0973—dc20   89-28044
                                                                              CIP

FIRST PRINTING, 1990

Sage Production Editor: Diane S. Foster

CONTENTS

PREFACE

In an earlier book, *Changing the System: Political Advocacy for Disadvantaged Groups,* Dluhy (1981a) argued that political advocacy was one of the most frequently ignored skills of practice in social work and the human services professions. Nine years later, this argument can still be made without any modification. That earlier volume devoted only one brief chapter to coalition building, which is the major topic of this book. Since the publication of *Changing the System,* many teachers and practitioners in social work and the human services have indicated that a book focusing on how to be successful at coalition building would be a helpful contribution, in light of the scarcity of public funding and the long-term shift away from societal support for human services; thus we decided to look into the topic in more depth, so that useful direction could be given to practitioners and educators interested in this aspect of political advocacy.

The successful use of coalitions is only one of the many skills needed by practitioners in social work and the human services as they strive to become successful political advocates for the disadvantaged, but it is a skill that is essential in today's political and economic environment. The untimely death in 1987 of Wilbur J. Cohen reminds us all how important advocacy skills are. Wilbur was the preeminent "coalition builder." The inspiration to write this book came largely from Wilbur's encouragement and, most important, the example he set for all of us in social work and the human services who believe that "programs for the poor need not be poor programs." He will be missed.

At the end of each chapter there is an exercise and guide for individuals and groups who want to expand their understanding of the key concepts discussed and illustrated in the chapter. As discussed in the first chapter, these exercises and group guides are designed to improve the ability of practitioners to reflect in action.

Finally, I would like to thank Sanford L. Kravitz and Armand Lauffer of the University of Michigan, coeditor of the Sage Human Services Guides series, for their patience and helpful editorial suggestions on earlier drafts of this book. Their guidance in the preparation of this volume has stimulated me to consider different and creative ways of presenting materials to readers.

—Milan J. Dluhy

Chapter 1

COALITIONS AS INSTRUMENTS FOR CHANGE

An important assumption of this book is that we are currently experiencing and will continue to experience a major societal trend in which there is a long-term shift away from public support for the human services. This diminishing public support is taking place despite continued interest in welfare reform and other policy changes. If health care benefits such as Medicare and Medicaid are excluded from the discussion of human services, the lack of support is even more apparent. Language such as the "privatization of services," "devolution of responsibility for programs from the federal government to state and local governments," "substitution of informal or family care for government-sponsored care," and "increasing and expanding the role of charity in our society for meeting human service needs" is being widely used. Overall, the major shift that is taking place is the decentralization of authority and responsibility for human services from the national government to more proximate local settings. At the same time, it is not surprising that welfare reform is aimed primarily at making the human services more efficient and accountable, not necessarily increasing the level of resources available for worthwhile programs. Expansion of the federal role in the human services is highly unlikely in the future; rather, it is anticipated that the emphasis will continue to be on the proper management of the remaining resources devoted to the human services.

With the severe cuts in human service budgets at all levels of government that have taken place in the past decade, we can anticipate even fewer public resources being available for human services in the future (Salamon & Abramson, 1985). While there is some debate about how long term this cycle of shrinking public resources for the human services will be, there is little disagreement that human service groups will have to join together, wherever possible, to leverage the use of current public resources more effectively (Humphreys, 1979). The "environment of scarcity" produces, among other things, organizational instability and uncertainty, reductions in personnel, and service reductions or losses in the quality of services (Hasenfeld, 1983). This environment of scarcity in public funding in turn creates a "politics of scarcity," so that groups and organizations compete with each other for a smaller and smaller part of the pie. This book focuses positively on a particular kind of politics of scarcity, that is, how human service groups can join forces and work together in coalitions in order to leverage government resources more effectively, generate new nongovernmental resources, and find substitute resources.

CONCEPT OF A COALITION

The concept of coalition used in this book is very unambiguous. Basically and in simple terms, a coalition represents a time-limited organization in which there is a convergence of interest on the part of a number of actors, both individuals and organizations, and an interaction around furthering these common interests (Warren, 1977). But coalitions have other characteristics as well. First of all, they are mechanisms for explicitly coordinating some or all of the actions of the members; the coalition is an organization of organizations (Wilson, 1973). This concept is sharpened somewhat by the additional identifying characteristic of a coalition—that its primary purpose is the achievement of political objectives in the public policy process (Dluhy, 1981b). In this context, the term *political objectives* refers to securing resources and other public policy actions from government. While some coalitions also serve other purposes—such as providing social experiences for members, disseminating information for professional and educational purposes to their members, and allowing members to make contacts and find new jobs—the political purposes are central. The political purposes of coalitions are always paramount, and they will receive particular attention in this book. However, most coalitions do pursue a range of nonpolitical objectives as well, and, therefore, this book will also illustrate the achievement of nonpolitical objectives. Nonpolitical objectives are primarily those objectives aimed at generating and developing nongovernmental resources. As will be pointed out in Chapter 5, the achievement of nonpolitical objectives can actually enhance the overall viability of the coalition.

Although some coalitions endure over long periods of time, they are, for the most part, temporary alliances and unstable associations of people and groups. Since goals are regularly altered, resources frequently shift, and relationships among people often change, temporary alliances in which coalition partners meet some other pragmatic or policy objectives are necessary (Boissevain, 1974). While many coalitions strive for permanence, a coalition is by nature an ad hoc instrument to exploit new resources in changing situations. When coalitions begin to take on a more structural order and exhibit characteristics of other types of permanent and formal associations, by definition, they are no longer coalitions.

In sum, a coalition is defined as a temporary alliance of groups and individuals who band together to achieve both political and nonpolitical objectives (goals). Since coalitions frequently form during periods of insecurity and instability, it is timely to focus on what we have learned from coalitions in the 1980s, since this has been—and the 1990s will continue to be—a time of major change in the level of public support for human services in the United States. Thus a frequent hypothesis identified in the literature is that instability and turbulence in the broader social and economic environment foster the use of coalitions (Weiner, 1984).

ADVANTAGES AND DISADVANTAGES OF COALITIONS

Each organization acting in its own interest will seek autonomy, will secure its own resources, and will carve out its own domain (Wilson, 1973). A strong case can be made for organizing small, narrowly focused groups that accept the premise of self-interested behavior (Olson, 1968). Small targeted groups with narrow objectives can be quite effective, and these groups, when successful, do not have to share the payoffs of successful action with any other groups. Nevertheless, under certain conditions, joint action by groups using a coalition frame-work is desirable, and the payoff is worth the investment of effort. In a general sense, when each organization alone is powerless or unable to change a public policy or some other set of circumstances in the community, and joint action can successfully alter the situation, then joint action is desirable. Self-interest dictates that when the payoff secured by the coalition exceeds the costs of joining and participating in the coalition, then joint action is desirable. When the payoff exceeds the costs of joining the coalition, self-interest or group interest is maximized (Hasenfeld, 1987).

In an interview, the director of a local social service agency, in discussing the merits of joining coalitions, stated:

> I am always looking at the costs and benefits of joining coalitions. I can't go to every meeting and I can't be a member of every coalition which asks for my cooperation. I have a simple formula. Does the coalition provide me with critical information I can't get anywhere else? Does the coalition allow me to network with the important community leaders? Do I share the goals of the coalition? Will joint lobbying by the coalition be more effective than my own personal lobbying? Can the coalition cause a change in important public laws? These are all benefits for me and I don't mind paying the costs. If the benefits do not exceed the costs, I send my assistant to the coalition meetings.

It is important in this context to point out also that a payoff does not have to be either immediate or direct. Many groups join coalitions because they may anticipate long-term or more indirect benefits. The critical issue is that those joining coalitions perceive that there are some clear-cut benefits connected to their participation. Finally, the actual payoffs secured by coalitions may benefit individual coalition partners to differing extents: Some partners may benefit more, others less. In the long run, however, an individual partner in a coalition must perceive that the overall benefits will exceed the costs of participation.

Coalitions also allow individual organizations to become involved in new and broader issues without the necessity of totally managing or developing those issues by themselves. Thus coalitions give organiza-tions greater power and influence over an issue than any single organi-zation would have working alone. They enable the mobilization of greater numbers of resources, and they bring a wider variety of effective strategies to bear on an issue. However, it is also true that coalitions can divert energy and resources from an organization, that coalitions may take positions contrary to an individual organization's interests or policies, that coalitions may use a slow, consensus-building process for decision making that may result in a weakened position on some issues, and that coalitions may, because of differences among organizations within them, be prevented from taking strong stands or moving as swiftly as possible on particular issues (Black, 1983). In short, coalitions have both advantages and disadvantages to their members as instruments of advocacy.

While some organizations and agencies or individuals may join coalitions for a variety of reasons, another important assumption of this book is that successful coalition behavior involves an ongoing assessment of the costs and benefits of coalition participation by a coalition's members (Hasenfeld, 1987). Because time and other resources are valuable and organizations have to prioritize the use of their resources, participants should continuously assess when and under what conditions involvement in a coalition pays off.

FUTURE CHALLENGES FOR COALITIONS

There are many challenging social and economic issues facing our society today at the national, state, and local levels. Increasingly these issues cut across the boundaries and domains of specialized human service agencies and organizations. When an issue becomes communitywide in scope and when the resolution of the issue lies beyond the capacity of a single agency or organization, then joint action is desirable and the formation of a coalition may become an important tool for social change.

In the current environment of scarcity, groups and organizations are often called upon to develop proposals for allocating fewer and fewer public dollars, even though the demand for services of all kinds continues to increase. For example, there is considerable discussion today about "rationing" health care, particularly for the aged. One argument is that we must balance our investment in children against our overinvestment in the aged by limiting the aged to essential lifesaving services that are funded with public dollars (Fairlie, 1988). Coalitions are now forming on both sides of this issue. Some seek more investment in children and other groups in need, while at the same time advocating a limit on the public funding of nonessential services for the aged. Other coalitions seek more funding for both children and the aged, but argue that this funding must go only to those most in need in both categories (Kingston, Hirshorn, & Cornman, 1986; Villers Foundation, 1987). This dilemma has been labeled the "intergenerational war." It presents a major challenge because it raises troublesome moral and ethical dilemmas for decision makers in the public sector (Jecker, 1987). Coalitions can cut across the separate and distinct interests involved in this and similar issues and thus develop temporary alliances aimed at achieving a common interest.

For example, because homelessness is also a complex issue that cuts across many agency and service boundaries, broad-based coalitions will be needed to deal effectively with this issue (Dluhy, 1987). The most troublesome aspect of homelessness is that the groups that are labeled as "homeless" are very heterogeneous. Very different needs characterize the subpopulations found on the streets. While the public would like a simple and straightforward diagnosis of and solution to the problem, the reality is that homelessness will continue to plague most large communities in the future (Marin, 1987). The challenge is to put together coalitions that can cut across agency and service boundaries so that the economic, social, psychological, health, housing, and other needs of the homeless can be met. Homelessness cannot be solved merely by building more shelters. The real issue is how we can develop more comprehensive approaches to the problem and how we can put together coalitions that support these cross-cutting and comprehensive approaches to homelessness.

Another critical and challenging issue facing our society is family violence. Broadly construed, family violence at a minimum includes child abuse and neglect, domestic violence or spouse abuse, and elder abuse. The issue of violence in the family cuts across numerous agency and organizational domains. Is it a mental health problem? A public health problem? An economic problem? An educational problem? A moral or ethical problem? A substance abuse problem? Coalitions will provide a framework whereby different perspectives can be used to address the cross-cutting aspects of this pressing and alarming problem.

Finally, the issues of the right to treatment and the right to service form yet another major challenge for our society. The courts have ruled that prisoners have a "right to treatment." Can we extend this concept to a "right to service" for the general population? Can a homeless person demand a "right to shelter"? If charity or the nonprofit sector does not provide shelter, then should the public sector be mandated to provide it? We have worked diligently to provide students with a "right to an education," certainly through high school. Do we want to extend this to college? How about the "right to emergency health care"? How about the "right to a job" or the "right to subsistence income"? Cross-cutting coalitions can help with the fundamental questions of what "services" are essential and fundamental in our society and therefore guaranteed by the public sector, as opposed to services that are desirable but not necessarily worthy of public entitlement.

If services are essential, they should become entitlements, and they must be universally available to everyone (Fallows, 1982). Our society has historically been characterized by its nonuniversal or categorical approach to service provision (Gilbert & Specht, 1974). As we approach the twenty-first century, coalitions will form to raise challenges about which services should be provided by "right" and therefore should merit government guarantees through public entitlement. Coalitions will become one of the major vehicles for raising and ultimately resolving these kinds of issues.

In summary, there are many important challenges for coalitions in the future. The intergenerational tension, homelessness, family violence, and the right to treatment or services represent issues that individual agencies and organizations have been unable to deal with effectively on their own. Coalitions, however, can facilitate the constructive action necessary to develop solutions to these kinds of problems.

LEADERSHIP AND COALITION-BUILDING SKILLS IN SOCIAL WORK

Social workers and other human services professionals have increasingly recognized the importance of becoming more effective politically (Dluhy, 1984). It may therefore be constructive to examine the development of coalition-building skills within the social work profession and to establish guidelines for practice from these experiences. Historically, social work has had a love/hate relationship with politics (Alexander, 1982). On the one hand, the profession has been committed to improving direct practice and the development of professional standards. On the other hand, within the profession many argue that its members should play a far more visible and political role within their communities and the larger society (Dean, 1977; Stewart, 1981). In this context, social workers must function as advocates for clients, and effective advocacy requires political involvement (Brager, 1968). Unfortunately, political content is often largely absent at the graduate and undergraduate levels in social work education (Haynes & Mickelson, 1986).

Political activity and involvement are still viewed largely as a matter of individual preference rather than as the intended outcome of social work education and training (Haynes & Mickelson, 1986). However, there is now some limited evidence that the helping profession of social work is turning more of its attention to leadership development (Brilliant, 1986). Even though leadership training currently has no prominence in the social work curriculum of most degree programs, there is renewed interest in the area. This interest in the acquisition of leadership skills includes the ability of social workers to overcome their sense of powerlessness based on their historical connection to disadvantaged populations. Even though the profession and professional education in social work have increased their emphasis on program and financial accountability, management, budgeting, and program evaluation in the past 20 years, training in leadership and political action has not received much attention since the 1960s (Brilliant, 1986). One critical challenge for social work and other human services professions is to focus more attention on leadership training, particularly training in political advocacy. A critical skill in political advocacy training is the ability to develop and use coalitions to achieve desired outcomes.

REFLECTION IN ACTION:
GUIDELINES FOR PRACTICE

The audience for this book is made up of the members of the professions interested in political advocacy and how it can be used to achieve social change in the human services. Educators and practitioners in social work, health services, criminal justice, law, public administration, nursing, and the like need more exposure to the art and science of coalition building. Many leaders in these professions aspire to be creative, to take risks, and to promote innovation (Garner, 1989). The use of coalitions is one of the major instruments available to these leaders, and therefore this book focuses on how to use coalitions as instruments for change.

Throughout, we focus on how professionals can learn about what works and what does not work in the area of coalition building. From their own practice and the practice of others, when practitioners reflect in action, they develop concepts to guide their actions (Schon, 1983). The case materials presented in this book allow this kind of reflective inquiry. Knowledge for practice can be derived by constructing new knowledge and insight based on examining practicing coalitions. In this context, the case materials and the exercises at the end of each chapter allow readers to test their abilities to use reflective inquiry to develop new insights into coalition behavior.

To date, much of the literature on coalition building has been largely theoretical and conceptual. Even though the literature does not reflect consensus about a single, overarching theory, there has been a substantial amount written that focuses on game theory and its applications to coalitions, social psychological models of coalitions, and political or power models of coalitions (Hill, 1973; Kahan & Rapoport, 1984; Murnighan, 1978). Unfortunately, there have been only a few descriptive studies of coalition formation, and the field shows a virtual absence of research on practicing coalitions (Stevenson et al., 1984). I attempt to fill this gap by presenting case materials on actual coalition behavior in order to develop a set of guidelines that educators and practitioners can use as they enter the political environment through participation in coalitions. Practical advice derived from case studies and reflective inquiry together with conceptual and theoretical insight that is derived from reading the literature can lead to more effective collective action.

In the end, coalitions can provide one of the most effective tools available for professionals to use in achieving their objectives when faced with power configurations that might otherwise appear intimidating. The principal message of this book is that coalitions must be viewed realistically and practically in terms of individual and group resources; a beginning point is to reflect in action carefully and then abstract guidelines that can guide practice. In order to facilitate reflection in action, we provide exercises and group discussion guides in each chapter. Readers are encouraged to use these exercises and discussions in staff development sessions, workshops, and other group meetings where professionals are exploring the further development of their advocacy skills.

ORGANIZATION OF THE BOOK

In order to abstract the best guidelines for practice and improve the ability of practitioners to reflect in action, we have organized this book in the following way. Chapter 2 briefly reviews the experiences of 13 different coalitions. A typology of coalitions is introduced that serves as a guide for reading about these different kinds of coalitions. The chapter poses a set of questions that can be asked about coalitions in the human services. This is the first opportunity for readers to test their ability to reflect in action.

Chapter 3 describes how to organize and develop a coalition. This discussion provides a framework for those interested in the development and maintenance of coalitions. Chapter 4 isolates and compares the different strategies and tactics that coalitions use in practice. Chapter 5 continues the discussion of strategies and tactics, but the focus is on activity aimed at achieving nonpolitical objectives.

The final chapter summarizes the major guidelines for practice by having the reader examine a hypothetical case describing a coalition and then answer a set of questions about coalition behavior. The examination of this case challenges the reader to reflect in action and apply the knowledge presented in the earlier chapters. The chapter also raises some broader conceptual issues that the academic and theoretical community can work on in the future.

A NOTE ON METHODOLOGY

Through participant observation and interviews, we have accumulated detailed knowledge of 13 different coalitions that have operated at the national, state, and local levels. We conducted 25 formal interviews with various members of these coalitions (the questions covered in the interviews are included in the Appendix). Quotes from these interviews appear throughout the book to illustrate major themes or points. These coalitions do not represent a statistical sample and therefore they may not necessarily be representative of all the different types of coalitions in the human services. This was not meant to be a tightly designed empirical study of coalitions. Rather, this is an exploratory study of practicing coalitions. The hope is that the guidelines for practice identified in this book can be studied in a more systematic and representative fashion in the future. The purposes here are to describe and gain insight into coalitions and to provide direction for practitioners and educators who want to be involved in coalitions.

SUMMARY

Coalitions are valuable instruments for change that can be used by professionals in the human services to achieve both political and non-political objectives. Even though participation in coalitions has to be evaluated carefully by each partner in the coalition, joint action is frequently the most fruitful course of action when cross-cutting issues arise in a community. Practitioners are urged to reflect in action as they read the book, do the exercises, and participate in group discussions following the guides presented in the chapters. Skills in coalition building will be essential for human services professionals in the anticipated austere fiscal environment of the future.

EXERCISE FOR PRACTITIONERS

Below are descriptions of ten different client groups, with problems that practitioners often encounter.

(1) teenage males, runaways from home and/or status offenders, truants, drug abusers, those on probation for breaking and entering, families no longer interested in helping

(2) the chronically mentally ill, over 55 years old, in and out of hospitals, heavily medicated and exhibiting bizarre behavior, families disinterested in helping

(3) children up to age 13, history of foster placements, generally poor academic records, some truancy, often minority, some with learning disabilities or emotionally impaired

(4) males 30-45 years old, no families, previous institutionalization for mental health reasons, substance abusers, irregular employment behavior, numerous physical health problems, periodic contacts with law, frequently homeless

(5) adult males all ages, spouse abusers, child abusers (physical), substance abusers, on probation for attacks on wife and/or children, middle-class backgrounds with secure jobs

(6) females 70 years and over, living alone in own homes, low income levels, living in older neighborhoods, homemakers, never worked, chronic health problems, homes in need of repair

(7) teenage females, promiscuous, from broken homes, most sexually abused by fathers, no job skills, dropped out of school before the age of 16

(8) males and females 65 years old and over, all income levels, healthy, bored, retired and dissatisfied with retirement, transportation available

(9) veterans (Vietnam), in 40s, irregular employment behavior, substance abusers, periodic violent episodes, frequent problems with police, sympathetic families

(10) females with young children, not married, poverty-level income, irregular employment behavior, few job skills, low motivation to acquire new skills

In a group discussion, try to arrive at some consensus on the following questions:

- How can I present each group to the community so that the community will be sympathetic and eventually fund programs to help the group?
- What image of the group needs to be projected?
- Which group is the easiest to advocate for? Which is the hardest? Why?
- Why are some groups hard to advocate for? Why are other groups easy to advocate for?
- Who are key individuals and groups in your community who would join a coalition to help each client group?
- Why did you select these individuals and groups?
- What were your reasons?

Chapter 2

A TYPOLOGY OF COALITIONS

Political action through coalitions at the community, state, and national levels is the focus of this chapter. Political action is undertaken by agencies or organizations in the human services, by professionals who are either an integral part of these agencies/organizations or who operate independently and autonomously, and by people in the community who act as individuals or as agents for groups that are not directly involved in the human services (Burghardt, 1987). One of the central dilemmas for coalition members is whether they represent themselves, their profession, their agency, or some other group in the community.

What "hat" is a coalition member wearing when he or she joins and works in a coalition? Almost all of the interviews with coalition members conducted in our exploratory study identified this as a central dilemma for coalition members. While there is no clear-cut or simple response to the question of who a coalition member represents, a sensitive practitioner must continuously be aware of this dilemma. For example, if the coalition takes a controversial stand on an issue, does the member have to check back with his or her agency board or executive director? How about checking with that agency's major funding source?

Many of the interviews with coalition members suggested that coalitions often move very slowly and take very conservative positions on issues because individual coalition members indicate they must check with or touch base with their different reference groups before political

21

action is possible. It would be simpler, as one coalition member indicated, "if everyone came to the coalition strategy meetings as a citizen and an autonomous individual, rather than representing someone else's interests." The reality of most coalitions is that they are conglomerations of organizations, groups, and professions; for this reason, concerted political action, while possible, requires adroit leadership and an internal consensus-building process within the coalition if that coalition is to operate successfully.

Stop and Think

Whom do you represent when you go to coalition meetings? Do you have to check with anyone before you take a position within the coalition or endorse a position of the coalition? On which issues are you free to act and on which do you have to touch base with the group that you represent?

Most coalitions are often preoccupied with several central concerns. First, how can a coalition respond to a crisis or dramatic event? For example, existing financial resources may be suddenly jeopardized or a dramatic event may have taken place and there may be demands from the public that organizations and agencies must act together for the common good. Second, how can a coalition be goal seeking and proactive and still achieve mutually agreed-upon policy, program, or service objectives? Third, how can a coalition protect the various bases of its membership or how can survival or self-maintenance objectives of its individual members be preserved? Coalitions work by pooling resources to preserve the status quo, to support social change proactively, or to respond, in the short run, to a crisis or dramatic event (Hasenfeld, 1987). The most important task for any coalition is to demonstrate to the larger community that it is the most legitimate group in the community that is capable of resolving an issue or problem. Once a coalition loses its credibility as the major force in the community speaking out on a particular issue or problem, it is very likely that it will go out of existence. Since most coalitions are temporary alliances, timing is critical. Coalitions must be able to respond rapidly, even if only symbolically, to communitywide concerns, or they will lose their reason for being.

A TYPOLOGY OF COALITIONS

In my experience, three questions about coalitions are often raised by practitioners in the community:

(1) Should coalitions have only one mission at a time or can (and should) they be multimission in focus?

(2) Should coalitions remain short term and ad hoc in nature or should they adapt and strive for permanence? In short, should coalitions take on more of a structural order and a long-term focus?

(3) What should the group base of the coalition be? Should it be professionally based, agency based, community based, or have a mixed base with some combination of all three?

Table 2.1 responds directly in the form of a typology of coalitions. First, what is the focus of the coalition? Is the focus a single issue or narrow client focus or is the focus multi-issue, even though the issues may all be identified with a single client or problem group, such as children, the aged, housing, or health? Coalitions that cut across client, service, and program lines, like the intergenerational coalition mentioned in Chapter 1, are clearly multi-issue. Single-issue coalitions tend to be ad hoc, but even they can persist over time, especially if the issue remains as a major community or societal concern. Thus one central dimension of a useful typology of coalitions is the focus of the coalition.

The second dimension of the typology presented in Table 2.1 is the group base of the coalition. The issue here is whether a person joins the coalition to further the interests of his or her profession or agency or as a member of the broader community. The nature of the coalition membership is always critical to its ability to achieve its objectives. In general, agency-based coalitions appear to be more interested in preserving the status quo, surviving, or protecting their funding base. Professionally based coalitions, in general, appear to be most interested in the development of new programs, especially programs that professionals will be involved in implementing. Community-based coalitions appear to be the most supportive of proactive social change, especially social change that is responsive to a crisis or some dramatic event. Many coalitions have mixed bases of membership, and this characteristic often contributes to the development of factionalism within the coalition.

TABLE 2.1 Typology of Coalitions

Group Base of Coalition	Focus of Coalition	
	Single Issue or Narrow Focus	Multi-Issue or Broad Focus
Professional or agency[a]	Bread-and-butter	preassociation
Community[b]	consciousness raising	prefederation
Mixed[c]	network	pre-social movement

[a]Individual joins coalition to further the interests of the agency or organization of which he or she is member. Personal or individual professional considerations are secondary.
[b]Individual joins coalition to further personal, individual, or professional considerations or altruistic goals. Agency or organizational interests are secondary.
[c]Motivations for membership and participation are mixed.

Using this typology as a guide, 13 brief case studies of actual coalitions are presented for illustration and examination in this chapter. They are organized into coalitions labeled *bread-and-butter, consciousness-raising, network, preassociation, prefederation,* and *pre-social movement.* Table 2.2 outlines some of the basic descriptive characteristics of each type of coalition; I recommend the reader study this table before reading the cases. There are illustrative cases in this chapter for each type of coalition in Tables 2.1 and 2.2 except the pre-social movement type. At the end of each case description, I present a number of questions worth discussing or thinking about. These questions will help the reader begin to focus on the more important aspects of coalition building. The cases and these questions should be examined carefully.

The issue of how structured a coalition can become before it evolves into a different form of social organization is also reflected in Tables 2.1 and 2.2, where three of the coalition types are designated as "pre." It is important to clarify why this prefix is used before we present the cases. This clarification will help to distinguish coalitions from other forms of social organizations, and this will make the typology more useful. The term *structural* refers to the degree of internal organization developed by the coalition. This might include things like developing bylaws, seeking more permanent funding to support a whole range of coalition activities, and organizing the membership into task or work groups that can achieve a wide range of objectives for the coalition.

TABLE 2.2 Characteristics of Coalitions

Characteristics	Bread-and-Butter	Consciousness Raising	Network	Preassociation	Prefederation	Pre-Social Movement
Selection and recruitment of membership	based on professional credentials and identification; by invitation; closed system; only key people or groups	loose; open system; broad base	loose; open system; broad base; community leaders and organizational heads	membership as a result of organizational affiliation	membership as a result of individual self-interest	loose; open system; broad base
Ideology/conflict	narrow ideological or value base	narrow ideological or value base	narrow ideological or value base	multi-issue	multi-issue	multi-issue
Resources	substantial if in-kind resources of agencies are counted	limited	can be substantial	substantial	substantial	substantial
Staff	in-kind support; rarely paid staff	volunteers; occasionally paid staff or interns	volunteers; paid staff common	volunteers and paid staff	volunteers and paid staff	heavily volunteer; some paid staff
Communications	regular and formal; meet as part of job responsibilities	regular and formal	frequent, both formal and informal	extensive	extensive	loosely organized; media driven

TABLE 2.2 Characteristics of Coalitions (Continued)

Characteristics	Bread-and-Butter	Consciousness Raising	Network	Preassociation	Prefederation	Pre-Social Movement
Longevity	long term, especially if personnel are the same	short term; when no issue on agenda, go out of existence	can be long term if coalition is successful	long term	long term	long term if agenda is changed
Issues	single issue or issues within narrow service area	single issue or issues within narrow service area	legislative; budget	model programs; budget; training; ethics	multiple issues; constantly changing	multiple issues; constantly changing
Organizational or internal structure	informal, but elite group of decision makers; bylaws and officers	bylaws and officers; informal, but elite group of decision makers	bylaws, officers, periodic meetings; annual conferences	very formalized and bureaucratized	loosely organized except during crisis	loosely organized except during crisis
Examples from chapter	Coalition for Community Care for the Elderly; State Alliance of Information and Referral Programs	Coalition for Missing Children; Coalition for the Homeless	National Coalition of Youth; SOS Generations United	State Alcohol and Drug Abuse; Coalition of Youth Services	Consumers Coalition; Coalition for Developmentally Disabled	Feminist movement; aging movement; civil rights movement; anti-poverty movement

Chapter 3 will identify more clearly how a coalition can develop the internal mechanisms that are necessary to sustain itself over time.

For example, a *bread-and-butter* coalition, which is narrowly focused on a single issue or client group and is composed of professionals and agency-based representatives, is described in the typology as a more temporary alliance. As it moves toward permanence and structural order while broadening its mission, it is called a *preassociation* in the typology. However, as long as the central mission of the preassociation continues to be the achievement of political objectives in the public policy process in conjunction with a number of other nonpolitical objectives that reinforce and enhance these political objectives and as long as this type of coalition continues to have representation from several professions and several agencies, it can still be identified as a coalition. However, if the preassociation loses its political emphasis and begins to be dominated by other kinds of nonpolitical goals, it may simply evolve into a more traditional professional association, preoccupied with questions related to practice, professional standards, or the educational needs of its membership. When the political purpose is no longer paramount, it ceases to be a coalition. In this case, we might just call it a professional association. Otherwise, more structural order, per se, does not disqualify it from being referred to as a coalition.

A *consciousness-raising* coalition that is community based and also focused on a single issue or client group is a temporary alliance. As it moves toward permanence and structural order, the question can also be raised as to when it ceases to be a coalition. Even though the term *prefederation* is used to refer to those community-based coalitions that broaden their focus and mission, members of the coalition do not relinquish their control to a centralized administrative unit. The membership does not become subordinate to a central authority. The confusion arises because historically many coalitions of local agencies united and formed compacts and set up separate centralized administrative units for resource allocation, and thus they became known as federations, community councils, welfare boards, and the like. In the typology used in this book, a prefederation is still a coalition regardless of its structural order as long as the political purposes remain paramount and the members of the coalition do not relinquish fiscal control to another body. It may seem a logical next step for a coalition to develop a formal compact for resource allocation, but when it does, it ceases to be labeled a coalition.

A *network* is a loosely coupled group of professionals, people from the community, and agencies and organizations who band together periodically around certain issues or because of the needs of specific client groups. Networks have political agendas, but their broad membership base makes concerted political activity difficult, although certainly not impossible. Many decision makers defer to networks, not necessarily because they have been directly lobbied by them, but because these networks, with their broad membership bases, constitute a serious political threat because they may become mobilized at some later point in time. A *pre-social movement* is an extension of a network in that the coalition broadens the issues it will work on and continues to plan for and then implement a whole series of organized activities aimed at achieving specific objectives. As long as the political purposes of the pre-social movement remain paramount, it should continue to be classified as a coalition. What may happen to many pre-social movements is that their specific political objectives become absorbed into and overshadowed by an overarching political ideology or philosophy. This ideology or philosophy can become so broad and encompassing that it may include a whole range of activities that go well beyond the narrow objectives and activities of the kinds of coalitions referred to in this book.

In this case, a social movement has formed when the ideology or philosophy becomes so global that the idea of a specific organization, like a coalition meeting periodically to develop and implement an agenda, is no longer important. Rather, a whole range of loosely organized and often spontaneous activities begin to take place in the community and the concept of planning and central direction through a coalition is of a lesser priority. Thus the aging movement or the feminist movement or even the antipoverty movement becomes so broad in focus and so encompassing in purpose that activity directed through a single coalition no longer describes reality. This typology focuses only on coalitions that have specific agendas for action that are directly connected to the advocacy efforts of their members.

In summary, as long as a coalition maintains a balance in its membership, retains the centrality of its political purpose, and does not bargain away control over resource allocation to a centralized and separate administrative authority in the community, it can be identified as part of the typology presented in this chapter.

BREAD-AND-BUTTER COALITIONS

COALITION FOR COMMUNITY CARE
FOR THE ELDERLY (STATEWIDE)

The Coalition for Community Care for the Elderly (CCE) is agency based. For several years, 50 program directors who managed community-based programs for the elderly throughout a midwestern state met regularly for professional in-service training. Each of these program directors had managed volunteer programs that involved older adults in community-based projects. While some individual programs received federal money, most relied on state money and local fund-raising campaigns. Training sessions provided skills in such areas as supervision, staff development, and fund-raising, but they also allowed directors to interact informally and become acquainted socially.

When the state experienced severe fiscal problems, the directors began to meet informally after in-service sessions to discuss how they could collectively influence the state budget and their own appropriations. They recognized their common problems of agency survival, and agreed to cooperate to maintain or increase their funding from the state. They began by electing officers, drafting bylaws, and developing a formal newsletter that was sent to all of the coalition's members.

The coalition was successful in maintaining current funding in its first year, and in increasing funding modestly in its second year. The CCE then reached a crossroads. Some coalition leaders recognized success and wanted to turn their attention to other pressing issues in the aging field. However, other members felt they had become too "political" already and they might compromise their professional status in their home communities, while yet others urged a broader and more visible "political" agenda and discussed the possibilities of hiring a part-time lobbyist and establishing an office in the state capital. The coalition remains viable today, meets regularly, and maintains effective internal communications. The question for this coalition is whether it should adapt to a new set of issues, reformulate toward stronger political action, or disband altogether. This coalition is at a new crossroads.

Stop and Think

If you were a member of this coalition, would you wait for another issue to surface that would stimulate the coalition to act, or would you recommend to the membership that a subgroup of the coalition be appointed immediately to develop an action agenda for the full group to work on? In answering this question, also ask yourself what types of issues besides budget issues would be of particular interest to you if you were a program director participating in this coalition.

STATE ALLIANCE OF INFORMATION
AND REFERRAL PROGRAMS (STATEWIDE)

The State Alliance of Information and Referral Programs (SAIR) is a spin-off of an existing state runaway network. When crisis line staff with a special interest in suicide prevention decided to begin to meet informally but irregularly, this coalition emerged. SAIR formalized its structure largely in reaction to action on the part of state agencies (i.e., human resources, education, and law enforcement) to develop statewide suicide prevention programs without direct involvement of suicide prevention service providers and professionals. Initial activities for the coalition had been conferences, training activities, and consultation with the state human resources agencies on programs for suicide prevention. The coalition moved cautiously in the development of its relationships with other groups, as it strove to strengthen its own organizational base first.

In two years, the membership increased to 20. Currently, the members are predominantly youth services workers who are employed in crisis centers or runaway shelters. None of the members is an agency director, and there are no members from the community. However, the members feel they represent themselves, not their agencies or programs. The coalition is in a beginning phase of development and is just now considering more direct political action.

Stop and Think

Do you think this coalition should expand its membership base to include agency directors, influential community leaders, and other professionals, or do you think it should retain its current membership base? What do you think would be the advantages and disadvantages of changing the membership base?

CONSCIOUSNESS-RAISING COALITIONS

COALITION FOR MISSING CHILDREN (COUNTYWIDE)

The countywide Coalition for Missing Children was specifically organized in response to a federal grant to develop such a coalition. As such, it reflects a substantially different type of coalition from others in this chapter because the impetus came largely from outside the community. It was an idea developed in response to a federal RFP (request for proposal) and its substantial staff support was almost entirely underwritten by an initial two-year federal grant. There appears to have been little compelling interest on the part of local participants in the missing children's issue (e.g., police, service providers, children's agencies in the county) before the grant was made.

The staff developed a program, an information system, and a conference plan. The initial conference drew only one-third of the expected agency participants, and only a few of these were at the level of authority to have an impact on new policy and/or programs.

A presenting problem for this coalition is that the issue of missing children is widely misunderstood. A large proportion of the problem is believed to be related to family abductions. Most local police jurisdictions see only a few cases per year, if any. The requirement of staff to participate in the coalition conference activity may have represented an inordinate disposition of staff time for a relatively minor (that is, infrequent) local problem. It is clearly not a high-priority issue for the professional staff of many local agencies.

The coalition development process in the county also experienced setbacks because of the absence of a high-level commitment from several important agencies. In response, the project now appears to have downgraded its emphasis on local coalition building, and it has recently shifted its priorities to a focus on the provision of crisis line telephone information and guidance to parents of potential and actual runaway and abducted children, thus becoming a repository of information about missing children services and producing educational and training materials. It would appear that with the ending of government funding and the lack of a compelling local issue, the coalition will have difficulty surviving. At this point, the coalition lacks leadership and focus.

Stop and Think

One important question for this coalition is whether it should wait for another issue or external factor to come along that will coalesce the group or whether the leaders in the coalition should start looking for a really compelling issue to work on. What would you suggest? Should they wait or take the initiative?

COALITION FOR THE HOMELESS (CITYWIDE)

The Coalition for the Homeless is a community-based coalition organized to help homeless individuals in a medium-sized midwestern city. After two cold winters and numerous newspaper accounts, concerned citizens and clergy met to discuss the issue of how to get homeless people off the streets and out of the public library in the winter. While the 25 members in the coalition represented diverse interests in the community, they did share a common objective: to get the homeless off the streets and out of sight as quickly as possible. Despite a broad consensus on this objective, the operational goals of many members of the coalition were not the same.

For example, some wanted to purchase a shelter, others wanted to set up a referral system that would place people in foster homes, and still others wanted to give the homeless housing vouchers to stay at local hotels. Coalition members met very irregularly, kept no minutes, and argued continuously. In the end, they were able at least to get the issue on the formal public agenda, and the city council finally allocated money ($80,000) to purchase and refurbish a shelter for the homeless. The coalition did not provide the solution to the problem; rather, it exerted the necessary pressure on others to solve the problem.

The coalition then disbanded, and, even though the community is still struggling with issues concerning the homeless, it has never met again. In terms of organizational dynamics, this coalition formed rapidly in a rather unplanned way, but when it got the issue on the formal public agenda and officials responded, it appeared to lose its purpose and it finally disbanded. It is questionable whether this same coalition will ever form again. However, another group interested in the homeless, with somewhat different members and different objectives, could form if there is another crisis in the future. Some of the previous members might join again.

Stop and Think

When coalitions agree on an objective but disagree on the means for achieving this objective, as illustrated in this case, would you try to organize a new coalition around the faction that agreed on both the objective and the means or would you disband the coalition and wait for a new issue to emerge that might be easier to organize around? In other words, when the original coalition failed to survive after the action taken by the city council, would you have urged those who agreed with each other to set off on their own even though the membership base would have been narrower and perhaps less powerful?

COALITION FOR THE HOMELESS (COUNTYWIDE)

Located in a large southern city, and with a countywide focus, a coalition for the homeless was formed that consisted of a loosely drawn conglomerate of health agencies, social service agencies, church organizations, organizations providing immediate direct services to the homeless (i.e., food and shelter), and the lower-level staff of several relevant public agencies. Although no senior-level representatives of city, county, or state government have participated, staff support was provided (in-kind) by a local health council. No leading members of the business community were participants in this coalition.

Aside from a one-day conference convened for educational purposes, the Coalition for the Homeless had been unable to agree on a prioritized set of goals and objectives. This was attributed to the disparate interests of the participants. Some of these interests reflected the desire to build additional and more permanent housing facilities, while others were concerned but watchful regarding the impact of any activities by the coalition on their own agencies and services. The conventional wisdom is that the homeless are transients and therefore without franchise. While no high-level elected political leader in the community has taken a serious interest in the problem of homelessness, it is also the case that each relevant government jurisdiction in the area has passed the buck on up the line, and the coalition has not been able so far to gain any political or broad-based community support for funding.

It appears that the coalition has remained together out of shared human concern, but it has been unable to unite effectively around a common program. The homeless are relatively invisible in the community and do not congregate regularly in areas where the "average citizen" will see them. A warm climate in the city precludes a great deal of sympathy for the homeless, since the local media rarely draw attention to this group.

The major challenge for the future is to overcome apathy in the community. Currently, the attitude is "Out of sight, out of mind." No community leaders have made this issue part of their own political agendas. The lack of leadership and a clear focus have contributed greatly to the inability of the coalition to be a more potent force in the community.

Stop and Think

Is it necessary to involve high-level community leaders such as elected officials, religious leaders, and business executives in a communitywide coalition in order for it to be successful, or can service providers and other professionals who are not representative of the highest levels of influence and power within the community form the nucleus of a successful coalition?

NETWORKS

NATIONAL COALITION OF YOUTH PROGRAMS (NATIONAL)

This coalition deals with issues of youth and families at the national level. It is a loose organization of 800 individuals and organizations interested in a broad range of issues affecting youth and their families. It has been involved in issues relating to juvenile justice, runaway and homeless youth, missing children, and youth rights since the early 1970s. While the coalition formed initially in reaction to the passage of federal legislation that funded delinquency prevention programs for juveniles, in recent years it has become involved in a wider variety of youth and family issues.

Although the membership is diverse in geographic composition, the predominant number of members run residential programs for runaway youth across the country. However, the coalition has numerous factions whose operational goals conflict with positions taken by the national coalition. As yet, no major issue has split the group enough to force members to join other coalitions.

With success has come a degree of bureaucratization—formal by-laws, officers, paid staff in Washington, computer-based telecommunications systems for the members, quarterly newsletters, and an annual policy symposium that adopts formal and written policy positions. Resources are now available so that the coalition can expand its activities. Despite internal factional conflicts, the coalition has survived for 15 years and appears headed toward permanence. According to some, the success of the coalition and the stabilization of its organization and resources have given it a more conservative and narrow agenda in Washington. Bureaucratization has altered its short-term ability to respond to crises or pressing issues in the youth and family field. In fact, the coalition has failed on a number of occasions to take stands on controversial issues that affect its membership. Lobbying for more program and training funds has been the major goal of the coalition for the past decade. When it has taken on other issues, it has been ineffectual.

Stop and Think

Should this coalition continue to try to move beyond its narrow agenda of lobbying for more program and training funds? Would it be wise for the coalition to tackle more controversial issues, or should it continue to stick to the areas where it has been successful?

SOS: COALITION TO PROTECT SOCIAL SECURITY (NATIONAL)

In the late 1970s and early 1980s, there was considerable pressure to reform the social security system, especially the retirement income part, which pays benefits out of the Social Security Trust Fund. The U.S. Congress and especially President Reagan appeared to be ready to reexamine and then reform social security in the early 1980s. Wilbur Cohen, former secretary of health, education and welfare and long-time defender of social security, was one of the major organizers of the SOS Coalition in 1980. It attempted to forestall any major changes in social security.

TABLE 2.3 Membership of SOS Coalition

Chairman	William W. Winpisinger
Wilbur J. Cohen	IAM
former secretary, Department of	
Health, Education and Welfare	Msgr. Lawrence Cocchran
	National Conference of
Secretary-Treasurer	Catholic Charities
William R. Hutton	
National Council of Senior Citizens	Dorothy Height
	National Council of
Associates	Negro Women, Inc.
David Crowley	
American Association of	Stanley McFarland
Homes for the Aging	National Education Association
Frank Bowe	Cyril F. Brickfield
American Coalition of	NRTA/AARP
Citizens with Disabilities	
	R. Jack Powell
Lane Kirkland	Paralyzed Veterans of
AFL-CIO	America
Jerry Wurf	Douglas Fraser
AFSCME	UAW
Loyal E. Apple	Grover C. Bigby
American Foundation for	Board of Church and Society
the Blind	United Methodist Church

This coalition successfully fought off all major attempts to reform the system in the early 1980s. While Congress made incremental changes to patch up the financial problems of the Trust Fund, fundamental reform of social security did not take place. SOS had some of the most powerful leaders in the country as part of the coalition (see Table 2.3). A dynamic leader, Wilbur Cohen, was a very articulate and knowledgeable spokesman. While the group is currently dormant, political leaders in Washington cringe at the thought of this ad hoc coalition being revived in the near future. SOS is not an offensive coalition— that is, it is not promoting change—rather, the coalition seeks merely to prevent any major alteration or reform of the social security system established in 1935. The major tactics used by the coalition have been direct lobbying of Congress members in Washington, testifying before congressional committees, and periodic letter writing and telegram campaigns.

Stop and Think

Is it easier for a coalition to organize against something than to organize around seeking some positive change? Are the strategies and tactics of defensive coalitions different from those of offensive coalitions?

GENERATIONS UNITED:
AN INTERGENERATIONAL COALITION (NATIONAL)

In the mid-1980s, there were many attempts by numerous organizations and individuals to create an "intergenerational war," whereby advocates for children and the aged would be forced to choose between using limited public dollars either for children or for the aged. The intrusion of generational factionalism in public policy debates caused about 30 well-known organizations in the human services to form a loose coalition in 1985 to defuse potential intergenerational warfare and in turn to promote an agenda that united and joined the forces of the generations to demand from the state (i.e., public policy) universal life-course entitlements for basic human needs (see Table 2.4 for the list of members). The coalition has met a number of times, but it currently does not have a clear-cut mission, nor does it have an active agenda for change. With such broad-based members, it is hard for the coalition to have anything except a symbolic agenda that educates the public to the fact that intergenerational tension is a myth.

The future of the coalition is unclear. No major or single individual leader or organization has emerged as a spokesperson. The coalition has little or no defined leadership, and it appears to be nothing more than a very loose coalition of groups without a leader or compelling purpose. The future viability of the coalition is in question unless a dramatic issue is able to galvanize the membership. No attempts to move the coalition toward permanence have taken place as yet. The membership appears content to play a rather secondary role in the national intergenerational debate.

TABLE 2.4 Generations United Members of Coalition

Cochairs
Child Welfare League of America
National Council on the Aging

American Association of Children's Residential Centers
American Association of Retired Persons
American Federation of Teachers
American Public Welfare Association
American Red Cross
Association for the Care of Children's Health
Association of Junior Leagues
Big Brothers/Big Sisters of America
Boy Scouts of America
Camp Fire Girls
Children's Defense Fund
Children's Foundation
Congressional Award
Family Service of America
Foundation for Exceptional Children
Girl Scouts of America
Girls Club of America
Gray Panthers
Institute for Educational Leadership
Lutheran Council of America
National Association of Foster Grandparents Program Directors
National Association of State Units on Aging
National Caucus and Center on Black Aged
National Conference of Catholic Charities
National Education Association
National Network of Runaway and Youth Services
National School Volunteer Program
Older Women's League
Travelers Aid Association of America
Travelers Aid International
Young Mens Christian Association of the U.S.A.

Stop and Think

What are the advantages and disadvantages of a symbolic coalition like Generations United? Would you belong to a coalition like the one described above? Would you go to its meetings? Would you pay dues or contribute financially to its operation?

PREASSOCIATIONS

STATE COALITION OF YOUTH AND FAMILY SERVICES (STATEWIDE)

As a coalition of service provider organizations that all receive federal funds for one purpose, services to runaway youth, the State Coalition of Youth and Family Services is loosely affiliated with a regional coalition and somewhat more firmly tied to a national coalition. This coalition is therefore a part of a larger, loosely articulated network of coalitions of service providers concerned with a particular population at risk.

At the time I examined it, the State Coalition was six years old. Stirred to act more vigorously when it began to work collectively to offset a potentially devastating cutback in federal funds for runaway youth programs across all the states, it found itself unable to affect the federal funding formula. Therefore, the coalition targeted the state legislature to lobby for state funds to replace lost federal revenues. The coalition has since moved in its focus to broad issues facing children and youth and has spun off another coalition that is specifically concerned with crisis network and suicide prevention issues.

The coalition's original constituency (those concerned with crisis services to runaways) has been broadened as its agenda has become increasingly professionalized. The agenda now is dominated by issues related directly to the regulation of professionals working in this field, the training and educational needs of these professionals, and specific program regulations that affect the organizations that deliver programs for the runaways. Support for the coalition's state office now comes directly from the state human resources agency. While the constituent service providers pay dues, the bulk of the resources for the coalition now come from contract support from the state human resources agency.

While such support may be assumed to raise issues of co-optation, participation by coalition members is deemed essential to maintain or increase the service providers' (coalition members') funding base. This coalition is becoming increasingly professionalized and agency based, as indicated above. It no longer is community based. Its agenda is also becoming less visible, and it rarely takes on bold issues. While it tackles many narrow program and professional issues in the youth and family area, these issues have less community appeal. The fear is that the coalition will become captured by its funding source and lose its ability to tackle controversial and timely issues. While the coalition has taken on a more structural order in terms of its activities, dynamic leadership has been absent.

Stop and Think

If you were a professional in the youth and family area, would this coalition be attractive to you? Would you join it or would you look around for a coalition that was not connected as closely to government (independent of government funding)? Do you think a coalition should have an independent base of support, or should it seek government or foundation financial support where there might be some strings attached?

STATE ASSOCIATION (COALITION) OF YOUTH PROGRAMS (STATEWIDE)

Representing a group of professional social workers who administer residential programs for youth in a southwestern, rural state, the Association of Youth Programs operates a statewide association. Formed initially as a nonprofit association, it adopted bylaws, elected officers, and met quarterly to discuss issues such as licensure and regulation of professionals. Association members appeared to be in agreement on a broad set of professional goals, especially the outcome of proposed changes in licensing and regulation in their state. When the state experienced budget cutbacks, however, association members considered the possibilities of taking more direct political positions on other issues.

Since then, the association has successfully lobbied for maintaining funding for youth programs in the state, and it has seriously considered additional political activity. Nevertheless, some members oppose involvement beyond narrow professional areas of concern. They advocate continuation of the earlier record of success, rather than a reorganization of the membership with a new, more politically oriented direction.

The communications system within the group has become more formalized, with a newsletter, phone bank, and written position statements on various issues. The association employs a part-time professional fund-raiser, and recently it discussed the possibility of hiring a paid executive director and recruiting student interns that would be housed in the state capital. While members join the association as individuals, it is clear that they represent agencies that run residential programs across the state. The current leadership continues to set forth a political agenda for the group, and, as long as the association is successful, it is unlikely to disband. It is moving toward permanence.

Stop and Think

What do you think should be the balance between political and nonpolitical activity in this coalition? Do you think coalitions can become too political? Will some professionals avoid joining or leave coalitions that are too political? Would you participate in a coalition that requires a great deal of political participation from you? Are there limits to the kinds of political activities in which you will participate?

STATE ALCOHOL AND DRUG ABUSE ASSOCIATION (STATEWIDE)

The State Alcohol and Drug Abuse Association, now six years old, represents an amalgam of two older groups, one concerned with alcohol abuse and one concerned with drug abuse. The organization operates as a coalition of social service agencies, professionals, and representatives of the social work profession from across the state. When leaders in both fields defined their interests as common, they chose to merge.

The new coalition presented itself as having a dual mission: educating and training professionals working in the field, and having an impact on the state legislature through technical consultation on laws and regulations and on appropriations for alcohol treatment and substance abuse. In addition, the coalition attempted to set standards for service delivery and the quality of treatment. The coalition now appears to have gained substantial strength and influence with the legislature through tactics that stress collaboration and united action. Private treatment centers in the for-profit sector have participated in joint training programs, but they have not been a part of the legislative action network. This is in part attributed to the belief that they are highly competitive for clients.

Dominated by nonprofit agencies and professional social workers, the coalition has developed effective fund-raising techniques through its annual conference program and through training contracts from the state. The staff consists of four full-time professionals located in the state capital. It maintains a very active and highly sophisticated communications network that supports both the social action and the education and training agenda. It has achieved many of its tangible goals in the last few years. It is clearly moving toward permanence and more structural order.

Stop and Think

How important is permanent staff to a coalition? What kinds of things can staff do for the coalition? What other kinds of things should the staff not be involved in and thus reserve exclusively for the members of the coalition?

PREFEDERATIONS

CONSUMERS FEDERATION (STATEWIDE)

The Consumers Federation was founded in 1971 by a state supreme court judge in an effort to build a broad individual-based organization for consumer education. Its early name was the Consumers League. After a period of time, the organization appeared to go out of existence. Its corporate charter was reactivated in 1977, and its headquarters was moved to another part of the state. The location was a conscious decision in order to avoid the direct association with liberals that were associated with labor organizations and senior citizens' organizations at the previous location. The organization has grown substantially in its more recent history by adopting a strategy of linking already-existing organizations primarily around self-interest issues and then gaining participation from both groups and individuals working on behalf of their own interests.

Much effort has been expended to create a sense of ownership and involvement on the part of the participating organizations. Program issues for the year are developed at the coalition's annual conference, where a broad consensus of the affiliate groups, which now number 125, have been able to establish an action agenda. In addition to the labor unions and senior citizens' groups, the coalition now has consumer organizations, immigrant associations, condominium organizations, and environmental groups as part of its membership. It views itself as a broad-based, multi-issue coalition of low- and moderate-income people.

The coalition, which now has an annual budget of over $800,000, views itself as having a broad issue base with multiple sources of funding (e.g., dues, fund-raising activities, and foundation grants). Professional staff operate very much behind the scenes and devote a substantial amount of energy to the training and education of constituent groups, both on issues of substance and on political strategy. The coalition is acknowledged to be one of the most successful broad-based state coalitions in the United States. It clearly exhibits many of the characteristics associated with moving toward permanence and structural order. Its main strength has been the ability to handle a wide range of issues over the history of the coalition.

Stop and Think

What are the advantages of having a coalition with broad-based membership? What are the disadvantages? How important are full-time staff to broad-based coalitions? Could this type of coalition survive without full-time staff?

COALITION FOR THE
DEVELOPMENTALLY DISABLED (COUNTYWIDE)

The Coalition for the Developmentally Disabled provides an example of long-term staying power without movement toward permanence and structural order at the community level. It includes service providers, parents, and independent professional and cause advocates. Service providers and cause advocates often act independently of one another, but they come together regularly for united action and for periodic information sharing. Originally coalescing around both human rights (i.e., protection of the rights of the developmentally disabled) and the need for smaller groups to join forces to gain increased funding, the coalition now operates without a formal structure or staff; however, there are sufficient structure and resources located within its constituent members to organize efforts when issues arise.

Individual members of the coalition represent largely middle- and upper-class white-collar professionals, and as such, they have ties by friendship or reputation and can gain immediate access to political leaders at all levels of government whenever access is necessary. The support of this middle- and upper-class level of lay leadership also provides private resources to sustain lobbying efforts, thus obviating a pressing need for formal structure to sustain fund-raising activities or for a professional staff to mediate. The coalition members, both professional and lay, have direct access to both legislators and the media as well as to a pool of skills among members that enables them to utilize information effectively in their campaigns.

The client group around which this coalition is organized presents continuing and long-range problems for the community. It is served by a well-organized but separate set of organizations that offers somewhat different services. The problem of the disabled also attracts parents who are middle and upper class as well as human rights activists and concerned independent professionals. The client group can be seen as dramatic in terms of appeal. The active coalition includes many people who have disabled relatives and understand the problem firsthand. This coalition will not go out of existence in the near future, and it is one of the more successful groups described in its community. This coalition illustrates that political success does not always require a formal organizational structure. However, commitment, a clear focus, and leadership have been very essential to the success of this coalition.

Stop and Think

What are the different ways coalitions can gain access to decision makers and other community leaders? Are paid staff necessary for a coalition to gain this kind of access? What are the major factors that account for access to decision makers and community leaders?

SUMMARY

This chapter has presented a typology for examining different types of coalitions. This typology is based on the focus of the coalition, its degree of permanence and structural order, and the nature and composition of its membership. Using this typology, five different types of coalitions were illustrated and critical questions for discussion were raised about each coalition described. In reviewing all of the cases, it is critical to remember that while there is usually a movement toward permanence and structural order within most coalitions, this movement is not inevitable, and there can be disadvantages to more structural order. Of particular concern is the fact that more structure may, in some cases, lead to less willingness on the part of the coalition to respond to timely and compelling issues.

These cases also illustrate how most coalitions struggle with staying narrow and focused on a single type of issue rather than broadening their concerns to a broader array of issues. There is a point in the life of most coalitions when they must decide whether to move ahead into other issues areas or disband. Leaders often help coalitions make this decision.

Finally, even though there are many different types of coalitions, the type of membership a coalition has is probably the most important factor that explains its specific agenda. Mixed-based coalitions do have a broader power and resource base to draw upon, but they are also harder to manage because conflict and factionalism are more likely to emerge. In short, successful coalitions can have different types of members, but they may also have narrow membership bases. Success is more dependent on adroit strategy and tactics and the ability to mobilize the members of the coalition than on the composition of the group. Since coalitions are fluid and ever changing, how coalitions adapt and endure over time is the major feature of coalitions illustrated in these cases.

EXERCISE FOR PRACTITIONERS

As pointed out earlier, each case raises some interesting questions to pursue about the dynamics of coalition building. These questions were presented at the end of each case. Now review all of the cases in a group discussion and identify, at a minimum, five summary guidelines about the formation and development of coalitions that can be used to improve the practice of successful coalition building. Summary guidelines will be reviewed again in Chapter 6 in a more comprehensive manner, but the group is encouraged to make a preliminary attempt to identify these guidelines. In isolating these guidelines, pay particular attention in the discussion to the factors that lead to the successful formation of coalitions, the major incentives that coalitions can use to attract new members as well as retain old members, and what coalitions can do to keep themselves together over time when there are indications that they may disband. To get started, here are a few examples of guidelines that can be identified from the cases presented above:

- Coalitions will be more successful if they have some type of formal organizational structure and method of governance in order to formulate and implement their goals and objectives successfully.
- The leadership of a coalition should be aware of and use a range of incentives to sustain participation in a coalition.
- Symbolic activity on the part of coalitions may not be enough; tangible successes may be needed periodically.

Chapter 3

DEVELOPING AND
MAINTAINING COALITIONS

The Coalition for Community Care for the Elderly, a statewide group described in Chapter 2, recently completed a retreat during which members assessed the activities of the coalition over the past few years. The retreat started with the membership identifying the most serious problems the coalition had experienced since it came into existence. There was considerable agreement within the group that the most serious problems for the coalition have been keeping the policy agenda specific and up to date and making sure that the group's political strategies and tactics were coordinated.

During the retreat, it was revealed that the membership had many concerns about the lack of clarity of the policy agenda. For example, there were complaints that the leadership did not regularly communicate with members about the policy objectives being pursued. Some said the leadership did not articulate what political strategies were being planned or might be used. You will recognize these problems as similar to those of other coalitions described in Chapter 2. The retreat further revealed that there were other less serious problems that nevertheless required addressing. Among other things, the group identified conflict among factions within the coalition, poor communication among the members of the coalition, unproductive coalition meetings, inability of the leadership to be decisive, and periodic turnover of membership. Members argued that coalition tasks not only were time-consuming but had no meaningful payoff. Anyone who has worked in organizations will also recognize this as a common problem. Coalitions, indeed, have problems similar to those of most organizations, but, unlike most social agencies and many business firms, they must continually strive for clarity and purpose and their members have a need to feel that their participation can have practical, tangible, and positive impacts on the objectives of the organization or agency they may be working in.

In this chapter, I will explore how to start and then maintain a coalition. I will focus on the ways to minimize organizational dissonance while maximizing organizational successes. As one of the leaders of one of the most successful coalitions described in Chapter 2 indicated: "There is a model for successful coalitions. The model is that issues are paramount, staff is essential, leadership is critical, and education of the membership is mandatory." Does this sound familiar?

Beyond the insight derived from examining practicing coalitions, it is important to have a more general framework for examining questions related to the development and maintenance of coalitions. The literature on social organizations, especially organizational theory, offers a useful framework for understanding coalitions. For example, the emphasis today in this field is on "open systems" approaches to understanding organizational behavior, where concepts like interorganizational exchanges, environmental constraints on organizations, developmental patterns, organizational evaluation and accountability, and participatory decision making are commonly used to analyze various types of organizations (Sarri, 1987). In order to place coalition development in a proper perspective, the approach is to refer to coalitions as organizations that go through various phases or stages of development. As will be described in the next section, the first phase is to establish the mission or purpose of the organization (Perlmutter, 1969). In this initial phase, *transformational* leadership is needed within the organization, to transform individuals and individual organizations into entities with a shared sense of purpose (Burns, 1978). Once a sense of purpose has been established, the system of daily interactions among the organization's members and between the organization and its external environment can be established. *Transactional* leadership within an organization is needed to manage these more routine interactions (Burns, 1978).

Any leader who seeks to become involved in the development and then maintenance of a coalition must be both a visionary and a manager (Garner, 1989). As an organization develops still further and goes through other phases of development, issues beyond mission and purpose and the internal division of labor within the organization become critical (Selznick, 1957). For example, issues such as how an organization can gain legitimacy in the community and procure resources, how it can negotiate with the external environment, and how it can initiate and implement change are equally critical to the development of the organization, and they will be touched on in subsequent chapters. This chapter, however, will focus mainly on the earliest phases of organizational development, in which the mission or purpose is established, an internal division of labor or organizational structure is put into place, and the organization initially seeks to manage its day-to-day existence successfully, especially by developing the ability to manage internal conflict. The remaining chapters in this book will use this same organizational framework to follow a coalition through its various phases of development while at the same time examining the types of techniques that can be used to facilitate the evolution of a coalition from a temporary alliance toward an organization that exhibits more internal structure and stability, and therefore more permanence. This developmental framework focuses on the opportunities, constraints, and options available as a coalition (organization) attempts to transform itself into an institution (Selznick, 1957). The process of institutionalization, during which an organization transforms itself, is well known in the field of organizational theory (Hasenfeld, 1983).

THE FIRST MEETING

The driving force behind the formation of most coalitions is the occurrence of a timely and dramatic issue. Without a clearly articulated and framed issue, the fundamental agreement or concern that is needed in a coalition of individuals and organizations will be absent. The challenge for most coalitions is therefore to take a single issue and organize around it, move on to another issue and do the same, and keep doing this successfully until there are a stable cadre of leaders, an organizational structure, and sufficient resources available for mobilization of the members regardless of the issue. Over time, most coalitions will inevitably move toward some degree of permanence and thus follow the common process of institutionalization identified in the literature.

However, in the beginning phases of development, most coalitions tend to strive for credibility first so that they can be perceived of in the community as the legitimate representative or authority to speak out on an issue (Selznick, 1957). In practice, this means that the first issue chosen by the coalition must have marketing appeal; that is, the issue must be characterized in a way that others will find compelling. For an issue to take hold in the community, the fire and enthusiasm demonstrated by coalition leaders in the beginning phases of development are often critical (Haggstrom, 1987). It is coalition leaders who must articulate a dramatic issue or crisis that galvanizes the community and demands a community response. As many of the case examples illustrate, in recent years, such galvanizing issues have included budget cuts, abused clients, needless deaths among children and the elderly, electricity shutoffs, heartless bureaucrats who fail to do their jobs, and lack of services for isolated and needy clients. Less dramatic issues, such as the need for a common information and referral system to improve service delivery, the need for specialized training for professionals who serve problem clients, and the need for computerized client data bases to improve planning and resource allocation, are more difficult to organize around because they lack broad, dramatic appeal.

Nevertheless, coalitions are advised, as they begin to develop, to pick the most dramatic issue first and then weave many of the other less dramatic issues into their agendas as they move ahead in a dynamic way. Those coalitions that do not pick the most dramatic issue first can be successful, but the expenditure of resources required will be substantial and the length of time that it will take to be successful will be considerably longer. The framing of the issues and the phasing in of these issues over time are central tasks for leadership in a coalition, and they are tasks that are more transformational in nature because they define the fundamental mission while enhancing the sense of purpose of the coalition (Garner, 1989).

The first meeting of a coalition is invariably crucial. Based on the case studies in Chapter 2, we have made a number of observations about the ways in which coalitions get started. First, professional or agency-based groups who are meeting for educational and professional reasons may decide to politicize their groups by adopting more openly political agendas. The more political the agenda becomes, the more likely it is that a group will either change its name or spin off a new group with a new name and new leaders. The membership of the spin-off group may overlap that of the original group.

This spin-off group is the second way in which a coalition may form. The other way is that a coalition can form from scratch. Here, a new group is formed and no attempt is made to link this new coalition to an existing group or to modify an existing group by setting up a spin-off. Groups organizing from scratch have the advantage of focusing on the issue of the day without worrying about preexisting agendas, previous membership interests, or leaders with particular vested interests. The disadvantage of forming a coalition from scratch is that start-up costs can be a deterrent. It takes time to bring people together and to make sure that they arrive at a consensus on goals or purposes. An issue must be quite compelling to get people to come to the first meeting of a new group. When preexisting groups are used as a vehicle for coalition formation, the initial meeting is often easier to arrange because a sense of mission may have emerged from earlier contacts.

Consider the following guidelines for a first meeting. The overall goal should be to establish an organizational framework that builds ownership and control while maintaining an open, flexible, direct-action focus (Staples, 1987). Coalitions are by nature dynamic. They must be capable of exploiting resources from a variety of sources. The fluidity of a coalition allows it to shift the ends of the group if new or other resources become available. Therefore, at the first meeting, the governance system of the coalition needs to be clarified.

A useful starting point is often to elect a *temporary governance committee*. This committee has the responsibility of determining the formal process for electing leaders of the coalition as well as providing a temporary forum for the discussion of strategy and tactics. This committee will stay in existence until a permanent governance system can be put into place. The second critical task at the first meeting is to establish the political purpose of the coalition. Because members of the coalition may be there for a variety of reasons, it must be made abundantly clear that the membership all fundamentally share the political purpose of the coalition. This means that the "buy in" of the membership must come at the first meeting. Dramatic issues like restoring budget allocations for programs, developing a strategy for getting the homeless out of the libraries and away from the schools, and developing an outreach strategy for connecting an isolated, ignored, and needy frail older person with an appropriate service program can easily mobilize a coalition to act politically. The key is to find a shared goal that does not require members to give up their individual, professional, or organizational or agency goals. If the issue is clear-cut and the solution simple, the expected results of successful political action are likely to be tangible. Everyone is likely to be happy; everyone wins— the client, the agencies, the professionals, and the community. Leadership at the first meeting should make sure that the political purpose is clear, yet phrased in such a way that the membership "buys into" that purpose. This can sometimes be accomplished by laying out preliminary political action steps for the membership.

The last critical task at the first meeting is to agree, if only tentatively, on the membership base of the coalition. Different membership bases are likely to generate different goals. Professional or agency-based coalitions tend to form around less dramatic issues, such as securing funds for training, developing improved information and referral systems, upgrading and monitoring professional standards, improving public education, and making reimbursement systems operate more efficiently. Alternatively, community-based groups are more likely to form around issues such as the adoption of new laws or regulations, securing new or increased funds for programs, protecting clients, serving clients with dramatic needs, or drawing attention to neglected persons.

In many coalitions membership bases are mixed, with agencies, professionals, and community residents coming together. Mixed-base coalitions can be difficult to manage, because their memberships often struggle with both the ends and means of the coalitions. While narrow membership-based groups are often easier to manage, they may be less effective because they may lack the broader political base of mixed-membership groups.

The first meeting should clarify the degree to which the coalition should remain narrow or be broadened. Because there may not be a specific answer to this question, making this tentative or approaching the issue as a preliminary discussion may take some of the edge off of disagreements. A preliminary decision can always be placed on the agenda for review. In fact, preliminary decisions demand more review. I have found that successful coalitions do not put off decisions; rather, they come to preliminary and tentative decisions about governance, political purpose, and membership base in their first phase of development.

Figure 3.1 An Organizational Model of a Statewide Coalition

DEVELOPING AN ORGANIZATIONAL STRUCTURE

Coalitions can use a variety of organizational structures to help accomplish important tasks. Figure 3.1 presents a model that emphasizes the clarity of tasks that most coalitions need to complete. This model stresses the coordination of these tasks. The model can be modified to accommodate different coalitions. Over time, most coalitions move toward permanence in organizational structure. In the organizational theory literature, this phase of development is referred to as "adding rationality and coherence to the internal management of the organization" (Perlmutter, 1969). Figure 3.1 therefore assumes a gradual evolution toward permanence through the development of an internal differentiation of tasks that will allow the organization to operate smoothly on a day-to-day basis.

At the core of this proposed organizational structure is the *advocacy strategy committee*. This committee should be composed of approximately five to seven people who should be prepared to meet regularly and to commit a considerable amount of time and effort to the committee's tasks. The members of the committee should be appointed by the head of the coalition or elected by the full membership. The committee then should meet on a regular basis to address the following primary tasks: development of the overall plan of action or set of strategies and tactics for the coalition, coordination of the various activities of the coalition's work or task groups, and maintenance of overall quality control or monitoring of coalition activities (Dluhy, 1984). In this context, *quality control* means the continuous evaluation of how the action plan is working. The committee should not get involved in specific implementation tasks; rather, it should assign tasks to different work groups so that it can concentrate on the action plan and its implementation. The strategy committee must be small enough to meet frequently because frequent interaction will facilitate consensus building and the continuity of strategy and tactics.

In the interviews I conducted, assessments by coalitions of their activities revealed that a common problem encountered by coalitions with no staff is that the membership may go off in different directions. The result is little coordination of activities and no plan of action. At a minimum, the strategy committee can be used to overcome situations where coalitions have no staff or where the membership is physically or geographically dispersed. Use of a group approach to decision making minimizes the appearance of elitism and directs the membership to a decision-making group that is then seen as an extension of the individual leader chosen by the coalition. It is essential that any designated leader of the coalition also be a member of the strategy committee. Finally, major issues or statements of policy should be discussed by the entire membership, and then they may take formal positions. Beyond this, the membership can delegate authority to the strategy committee to plan and oversee the advocacy effort.

The heart of the successful coalition is the work group. Work groups are goal oriented, and they are responsible for carrying out the tasks that need to be accomplished by the coalition. These groups are similar to the task-oriented groups discussed in the literature on small group behavior (Friesen, 1987). While there is no set or exact number of work groups that every coalition should use, it is helpful to review the types of tasks in which individual work groups could be involved. It is essential to establish early in the life of the coalition that work groups are to report on a regular basis to the advocacy strategy committee so that the committee can both coordinate and monitor the action plan. Each coalition can decide whether work groups are ad hoc or permanent. The key issue is that particular work groups should have responsibility for the major tasks associated with the optimal functioning of the coalition. In practice, coalitions use work groups differently, but the major tasks connected with the operation of the coalition are always performed, regardless of the division of labor. As a guide, six different work groups identified from a study of coalitions are discussed below (these are graphically illustrated in Figure 3.1, and are also discussed in Dluhy, 1984).

(1) *Long-range planning and forecasting:* This group keeps abreast of what other coalitions with similar missions in other communities and states are doing. It also develops model legislation and model service delivery programs, compiles statistics on services and client needs, reviews professional publications and research reports, and examines foundation and other funding sources for announcements of demonstration or community networking grants.

(2) *Talent and recruitment:* This group organizes and completes surveys of the membership. Its purpose is to determine the amount of time that the membership has available for the advocacy effort as well as members' particular skills. The survey can reveal the types of responsibilities that members are willing and able to take on. Such a survey can be periodically updated to provide the leadership and advocacy strategy committee with information that can be used to make assignments connected to the implementation of the action plan. The survey should also ask the membership to identify others in their communities or their agencies who would be interested in helping with the advocacy effort. Finally, after receiving instructions from the membership, this group actively recruits new members and is responsible for their initial socialization into the coalition. Since most coalitions have constant turnover in membership, this task is critical.

(3) *Communications:* This group is responsible for legislative updates, special mailings, and the organization of a telephone bank for internal (to the coalition) communication purposes. This group develops the most efficient way of getting information out to the membership and, when necessary, lets the membership know what they are supposed to do when a particular strategy or tactic is being used.

(4) *Special events:* Every coalition will use certain special events to reinforce advocacy efforts. The tasks of this group include planning and
organizing such events as fund-raisers, "legislative days" in the capital,
receptions and cocktail parties, conferences, training sessions, retreats,
and other activities to give the coalition visibility and credibility.

(5) *Monitoring and oversight:* On a regular basis, pending legislation, state
or local government budgets, recently issued regulations and guidelines,
and other policy or programmatic changes affecting the membership of
the coalition need to be reviewed and assessed to determine if a political
position should be taken by the coalition. This information should be
quickly passed on to the strategy committee and, when necessary, the
full membership. The monitoring group is absolutely essential because
it monitors the late-breaking news on issues to which the coalition must
respond in order to maintain its credibility. The group works closely with
the leadership of the coalition. It systematically and comprehensively
reviews the public agenda so that the coalition can stay on top of the
major issues and avoid a position of responding after the fact. It compiles
an inventory of the names, addresses, and telephone numbers of key
actors in the legislative and bureaucratic sectors who may need to be
contacted as part of the advocacy effort. In some cases, detailed profiles
of key actors should be developed; these in-depth profiles can be
furnished to members who will be making direct contact with them.

(6) *Media or public relations:* Among other things, this group drafts and
disseminates position papers, resolutions, news stories, and other materials advertising the coalition. It may hold periodic press conferences.
Also, sponsoring an event of major importance, such as a legislative day
in the capital, provides visibility for the coalition.

While the agenda for the work groups may be lengthy, the overall
objective is to get the coalition actively involved in tasks that lead to
optimal functioning. The exact number of work groups is less important
than the tasks they perform. Depending on the size and geographic
dispersion of the membership, different configurations of work groups
can be used. This model can serve as a starting point for developing the
organizational structure of the coalition.

A major issue with which a coalition must wrestle in its early stages
of development is whether it will hire paid professional staff or whether
the membership and perhaps student interns will serve in lieu of paid
staff. As a practical matter, the coalition may not be able to afford paid
staff until dues are collected, fund-raising efforts are successful, or
other sources of funding can be found. Interviews conducted with
members of the coalitions described in Chapter 2 indicated that in most

instances those coalitions that used paid staff were very satisfied with the outcomes. In only one instance did coalition leaders indicate that using paid staff was a mistake. As one coalition member we interviewed cautioned, however:

> It is better to use paid staff who have come through the coalition or who are products of one of the agencies connected with the coalition or who are at least members of professions closely connected to the client group being served by the coalition. The worst staff are professional lobbyists who understand politics but who do not understand the system that the coalition members are a part of.

ASSESSING AND EDUCATING COALITION MEMBERS

The development of advocacy skills is at the heart of coalition building. In working with coalitions directly, I have found the following skills to be the ones that effective coalition organizers regard as essential for active members:

- ability to do their homework and always be prepared
- strong interpersonal or group skills; persuasive personalities
- sense of timing in terms of exerting influence; knowing when to use pressure
- intense commitment to coalition goals; ability to act for clients or advocate for a social problem
- ability to compromise and negotiate; knowing when to make a trade
- perseverance; demonstrating the skills to follow up and follow through
- patience; demonstrating the ability to listen
- acting as a team player by being willing to go along with the majority of the coalition
- demanding and pushy; knowing when to push and when to back off

One way of assessing coalition members is to have them sit down and do a self-assessment of their own personal skills so that they can see where their strengths as well as their weaknesses lie. It often is helpful at this point to bring in an outside consultant or trainer to do advocacy training, especially around the philosophy of why the skills listed above are so critical to successful advocacy. Members can be encouraged to attend workshops run by the coalition or local universities, or sessions sponsored by advocacy groups, that stress acquisition of these skills.

The second approach is to do a survey of the tasks or activities in which members would be willing to participate. Usually the primary socialization of the membership will come through participation in one of the work groups described above. More specifically, members can be asked which tasks they would be willing to help with and how many hours per week they could spend on them. For example, they could be asked the extent to which they would be willing to get involved in the following tasks:

- making telephone calls
- writing letters or sending telegrams
- preparing written documents
- monitoring legislation, rules, budget hearings
- attending political strategy meetings
- testifying before legislative committees
- lobbying public officials directly
- fund-raising
- working in an election campaign for a local elected representative
- raising funds for a candidate in a state or local election
- giving money directly to a state or local candidate
- asking a fellow agency employee or board member to lobby for the coalition

After members have indicated their willingness to participate in the kinds of tasks mentioned above, it will be possible to determine which members are willing to perform political tasks as opposed to strictly organizational tasks, and the strategy committee can make appropriate assignments to work groups. For example, working for candidates in election campaigns, giving money to them or asking others to give them money, and doing direct lobbying for the coalition are very effective ways of exerting influence. Nevertheless, as reported in one of the cases in Chapter 2, many professionals often feel uncomfortable "getting their hands dirty" performing political work, although they would have little or no difficulty performing other tasks on the list above. Many professionals and many community people feel uncomfortable in crossing certain boundaries, especially when activity is perceived of as too politically partisan in nature (Dluhy, 1984).

The leadership of the coalition and the advocacy strategy committee must be careful in assigning coalition tasks so as not to offend certain members. Therefore, surveys of willingness to perform tasks can be analyzed carefully so that the underlying philosophy of members is always apparent. In practice, community-based coalitions, as opposed to professional or agency-based coalitions, are more likely to feel comfortable with political tasks. The problem of "dirty hands" is more frequently found in coalitions dominated by professional executives.

It is essential to have members buy into ownership in the coalition while at the same time keeping the process within the coalition open and flexible. The members should feel they can have an impact on the action plan and its implementation. It is strongly recommended that coalitions develop an ongoing socialization strategy for new as well as continuing members. Regular retreats, in-service training, workshops, and guest speakers not only serve to enlighten members, but also contribute to the seriousness of purpose of the coalition. Members can be helped to understand the mission of the coalition, how it operates in practice, and they can be shown how strategies and tactics used by other groups can lead to success. Continual education of the membership will improve the chances of their buying into the coalition. This emphasis on continuous reassessment of the members as to their reasons for participation is consistent with the general discussion in the literature of the costs and benefits of coalition participation (Hasenfeld, 1983). As one coalition leader interviewed indicated:

> You cannot just keep asking people to help with the tasks of the coalition, you have to convince them that they are the coalition and that they are in control of its destiny. They need to understand the issues, the people, and the process. This is what education of the members means and it pays off because the members stay and they eventually recruit others as well.

MAINTAINING THE COALITION: MANAGING CONFLICT

One of the central tasks of coalition leaders is "brokerage" (Boisse-vain, 1974). Since coalitions are by their very nature dynamic, leaders of coalitions need to know how to manage conflict, how to get coalition factions to work together constructively, and how to keep the agenda alive and active so that members do not lose interest. There is a great deal of literature that focuses on the participatory management style of leaders. Even though there are costs because of reduced efficiency and productivity attached to a participatory management style, the benefits of greater member satisfaction, improved decision making, more successful implementation of decisions, and an increased sense of control and autonomy by members is well documented (Friesen, 1987). Therefore, leaders who adopt a spirit of encouraging participation will be able to complement their attention to the more concrete tasks or goals of the coalition. The most extensive attention in the literature on leadership is, in fact, related to how leaders allocate their time to both task-oriented functions and functions that stress interpersonal and intragroup harmony (Friesen, 1987). Successful coalitions need to emphasize both.

One strategy that keeps the motivation level of members high is to move the coalition on to other issues after it has achieved the ends for which it was originally put together. One task of leaders is continually to manage issues so that the membership is occupied with achieving outcomes rather than squabbling about personalities within the coalition or arguing about other internal organizational issues. Pragmatic successes or outcomes are the best remedy for coalitions (organizations) that are experiencing either ideological conflict or motivational lethargy (Garner, 1989). As one coalition leader interviewed indicated:

> Sometimes a series of less important issues needs to be resolved successfully with tangible outcomes or decisions being made before more difficult and controversial issues can be tackled and ultimately resolved.

Successful management of conflict also includes continual awareness of the incentives for participation in the coalition. Adroit leadership can reinforce these incentives when members begin to lose interest or when conflict between members arises. At this point, leaders need to remind members why they joined the coalition. It is also necessary to stress to members that they may have joined the coalition for more than one reason. For example, the following are usually thought of as the principal incentives for participation in a coalition:

- ideological or symbolic benefits
- tangible benefits for the member's agency or profession
- tangible benefits for the individual
- social benefits for the individual

- enhancement of agency or professional reputation
- improvement of client situation
- civic duty or pride
- critical up-to-date information and knowledge about clients, services, or the broader field

The leaders within the coalition should periodically remind the members of the benefits of coalition membership and what the trade-offs for participation are (Hasenfeld, 1983). Conflict about which strategy or tactic should be used can be lessened if members are reminded that their agencies will benefit by successful coalition action. Alternatively, conflict about how the coalition is being run internally can be lessened if members are reminded that their agencies or professions will become more widely respected in the community if the coalition is successful. In both cases, pragmatic success can be presented as the desirable end that overshadows all other conflicts.

Finally, experienced coalition leaders indicated in interviews that certain practices of coalitions lead to more harmonious internal operations. These practices were reported as being widely followed by the coalitions discussed in Chapter 2, and they are also very compatible with the philosophy of participatory management discussed in the literature on leadership (Friesen, 1987). Restated as practice guidelines, these major practices are defined as follows:

(1) Find a place for everyone in the coalition.

(2) Avoid elitism in organizational governance.

(3) Keep issues in front of the members; have no hidden agendas.

(4) Avoid organizational rigidity; do not become too formalized.

(5) Rotate leadership positions or use a small but representative policy or steering committee (i.e., advocacy strategy committee).

(6) Use periodic retreats and other self-assessment techniques.

(7) Do not waste members' time; stress tasks with clear payoffs.

(8) Stress organizational and professional credibility above all else; downplay individual personalities.

(9) Design political strategies that allow maximum participation among members; encourage multiple rather than single strategies.

(10) Openly discuss covert political action in which members may be asked to participate, but that they may find objectionable.

RENEWING THE ENERGY OF THE COALITION

Frequently, coalitions lose their raison d'être. When this happens, the central mission of the coalition may be in jeopardy. Without an institutional embodiment of purpose, an organization may not be able to move on to its next stage of development (Selznick, 1957). When this happens, three strategies for renewal should be considered. First, there can be a direct appeal to the conscience of the membership—that is, the fundamental agreement that exists within the membership about the clients being served or the problems being addressed. This consciousness-raising effort may come in the form of a dramatic speaker from outside the community, a visit to an agency experiencing serious client problems, or a retreat where "soul-searching" is the stated objective. Reassessment of purpose, if done dramatically, can reinvigorate the membership.

Second, it may be time for the coalition to take a hard look at its membership base. Do the current members still have sufficient philosophical commitment to the coalition? If they do not, can new members be recruited? The recruitment of new members can stimulate new enthusiasm and energy.

A third strategy, if all else fails, is to move on to an allied or closely related issue. The move to allied issues can usually bring new members into the coalition. For example, a coalition on aging may move into working on homelessness issues, especially in the area of homeless elderly. Or a child welfare coalition might move into an aging issue, such as a mentoring program between unemployed youths and retired workers, in an attempt to take on an intergenerational issue. Or a coalition for more mass transportation for the poor might specifically focus on the disabled, handicapped, and frail in an effort to broaden the coalition. In these cases, the strategy is to take on a closely related issue and then reformulate this issue in a different context. If this can be done successfully, it offers the promise of recruiting new members.

As many interviews indicated, there are forces pulling the coalition together, that is, trying to make it tighter, trying to narrow its mission, or trying to narrow its membership. However, there are also forces pressing to make the coalition broader and more adaptive, trying to modify the type of issues the coalition is working on, trying to take in new members, and trying to redefine the coalition's mission. These conflicting forces contribute to making a coalition what it is—an alliance of groups and individuals who band together to achieve common objectives. Some coalitions remain temporary alliances, but others survive and move toward permanence. In this context, some coalitions are able to move on to another stage of development, while others are unable to do so (Perlmutter, 1969).

SUMMARY

At the beginning of this chapter, it was asserted that the one model for success in organizing a coalition involves the following: keeping issues paramount; making sure there are adequate staff and/or members to complete coalition tasks; selecting leaders who are visionary, flexible, and able to manage conflict; and educating the membership so that they buy into the agenda of the coalition. In organizing a successful coalition, a great deal of attention must be paid to the beginning stages of organizational development and especially the first meeting of the coalition. It is at this first meeting that fundamental issues of governance, purpose, and membership base are established, and these issues shape the major character and mission of the coalition.

Coalitions will vary in the specific internal organizational designs they use, but successful coalitions must pay attention to these fundamental tasks: long-range planning; recruitment of members; communications within the coalition and between the coalition and others; the design of special events; the monitoring of legislative, bureaucratic, and fiscal changes affecting the coalition and its members; and media/public relations. It is also true that the leadership in the coalition must take on the responsibility of managing conflict within the coalition and maintaining its presence in the community as it strives for permanence in organizational structure. In short, coalition leaders need to emphasize both the task-oriented and interpersonal functions of the group.

Renewal of purpose or mission is always just around the corner. Coalitions must accommodate renewal by reestablishment of purpose, by changes in membership base, or by broadening their focus to other closely related issues. The coalition is a dynamic instrument to be used to achieve change, and without an emphasis on renewal, coalitions may be unable to move to another stage of development.

Organizing a successful coalition is a blend of instinct, a good sense of organizational practice, and an unfaltering commitment to change. Only when the members choose to abandon this instrument will it cease to exist. Many coalitions, through accommodation and adroit leadership, have been able to move in the direction of permanence of organizational structure, although the point of this book is that permanence of organizational structure is not necessary for short-term success, but it may be desirable for achieving a broader set of goals in the human services. Leadership constantly surfaces in discussions of organizational development, and it is certainly true that coalition leaders, like other leaders of organizations, will need a blend of human, conceptual, and technical skills to be successful (Katz, 1988). Leaders are both visionaries and managers.

EXERCISE FOR PRACTITIONERS

Pick an important community problem in which you are interested and for which there is currently no existing coalition seeking change. Set up the first meeting for the new coalition. Who will you invite and what will be the agenda for this first meeting? Schedule a second meeting and detail the approach you will use to govern the organization for the next year. Remember to indicate how the members will be involved and what they will do in the coalition. This will be your initial plan of action for getting started.

Finally, given the importance of leadership to the success of a coalition, identify five specific skills (not traits) that you would like the first leader of the coalition to have. Write a job description of no more than one page for the first coalition leader. Critique this job description in a group discussion.

Compare your plan for the coalition with other members in a group discussion. Try to arrive at a common set of practice guidelines after the group reviews each person's plan and job description.

Chapter 4

SELECTING COALITION
STRATEGIES AND TACTICS FOR
INFLUENCING PUBLIC POLICY

This chapter emphasizes coalition strategies and tactics related to achieving political goals in the public policy process. The next chapter will cover strategies and tactics related to achieving nonpolitical goals in the community. The key point of this chapter is that the leaders of a coalition need a *plan of action*. This plan of action includes activity aimed at goal attainment such as planning, directing, innovating, and procuring government resources. As a coalition moves to its next stage of development, it becomes even more concerned with goal attainment and less concerned, relatively, with organizational maintenance and control (Patti, 1983). We focus on the attainment of political goals first. Effective leaders of successful organizations are viewed in the literature as active participants in the political contexts within and among organizations rather than just as "bureaucratic technicians" who are able to manage routine tasks (Sarri, 1987). Drawing from the interviews conducted with coalition members and examining the literature on strategies and tactics, I outline an approach to strategy and tactic development that emphasizes political advocacy.

All coalitions need clear-cut *strategies*. In the broadest sense, strategies define what the coalition is. Strategies encompass the purposes, policies, programs, actions, and decisions of the coalition (Bryson,

1988). In the context of this chapter, strategies form the bridge between the coalition and its environment; they typically are developed to deal with critical issues and they outline the coalition's response to fundamental policy choices. Strategies determine the ways in which coalitions mobilize resources in order to achieve goals (Checkoway, 1987). Strategies enable coalitions to look ahead and anticipate alternatives, but they must also be technically workable and politically acceptable.

If strategies connect rhetoric, choices, and actions, then *tactics* can be defined more narrowly as short-term adaptive actions and reactions that are used to accomplish goals. Tactics are the specific actions taken by coalitions. The more closely connected tactics are to the broad strategies of the coalition, the more likely it is that these tactics will be effective tools for the achievement of the overall goals of the coalition.

Another critical term used in this chapter is *approach*. The approach of the coalition is the method it uses to accomplish something, or, put another way, the regularized and systematic way that the coalition goes about accomplishing its objectives. Coalition *style* refers to the way in which the coalition expresses itself through language, face-to-face interactions, and other forms of coalition behavior. It is the style of presentation that gives the coalition much of its identity in the community. The key concepts to which coalitions must pay attention as they strive for success are therefore strategies, tactics, approach, and styles.

A plan of action combines these concepts and does so by making a conscious attempt to link these concepts together so that they all reinforce one another. Successful coalitions are able to generate rational and feasible strategies that are then closely integrated with the tactics used by the coalition, the approach developed to accomplish the goals of the coalition, and the style adopted by the coalition to convey its message. Without a plan of action to link these activities, coalitions will flounder and be less efficient as they attempt to achieve both their political and nonpolitical goals.

SELECTING COALITION STRATEGIES

It is important that strategies be consistent over time. If coalitions are not consistent about what they say, what they pay for, and what they do, strategies will be more prone to failure (Bryson, 1988). The establishment of strategies should therefore be deliberative, and a broad consensus about them should be developed within the coalition. Without clarity about strategies, coalition effectiveness will suffer. Consistency of strategies will come with the continuity in membership and leadership that is developed over time within the coalition.

There are three aspects of strategies that need elaboration: goals, levels, and time frames. For example, the broadest goal of many coalitions is to have input into legislative, bureaucratic, and judicial processes so that tangible outcomes can be achieved in the public policy process. However, in order to have effective input, a coalition may need first to politicize its membership so that when tactics are employed, the members of the coalition will willingly participate. Additionally, many coalitions often do not gain access to legislative, bureaucratic, or judicial processes until the coalitions have credibility and visibility in the community. Thus all three goals may need to be achieved for a coalition to be successful. It may be necessary for a coalition to identify a wide array of goals initially, and then organize them according to how they will be pursued.

As illustrated by the case studies in Chapter 2, a coalition may need to spend a year or so just politicizing its membership, so that when more substantive goals (e.g., legislative programs, special funding requests, or government rule changes) are established, the membership will be ready to get involved in political action to support these efforts. Politicizing members may not be enough, however; it may also be necessary first to spend time enhancing the credibility and visibility of the coalition in the community by deliberately achieving nonpolitical goals. (The achievement of nonpolitical goals will be discussed in the next chapter.) Until decision makers trust the coalition and perceive it as a legitimate entity within the community, any political action it may achieve may be inconsequential. Putting these concepts together, adroit leaders in the coalition will need to think in organizational development terms—that is, how they can phase different goals and activities into the coalition over a period of time. Thinking conceptually about this kind of organizational development process is consistent with the literature on leadership in the human services mentioned earlier (Perlmutter, 1969; Selznick, 1957).

The phasing in of goals leads to the issue of time frames. It is not surprising that many coalitions, like other organizations, separate short-term goals from long-term goals. In the short run, or for the first year or so, emphasis on the politicization of the membership and improving the credibility and visibility of the coalition may consume most of the coalition's time and efforts, so that down the line the public policy process can be affected in a specific and tangible way. It may even be the case that in the long haul—say, over the course of five years—the coalition may even want to try to capture the policymaking process by having some of its members placed in formal positions of power.

The challenge for leadership within the coalition is not only to establish goals, but also to prioritize them so that a time frame for phasing them in can be established. It is interesting to note that many decision makers find it easier to put off or turn down groups they see only once a year, but they have more difficulty turning down groups who consistently lobby and make their presence known in the community. The continuity and consistency of the coalition will pay off in the long run when decision makers come to trust certain coalitions as the most legitimate and credible representatives of client groups or other identified groups concerned with social problems.

Ultimately, decision makers want to be able to turn to credible coalitions for advice on public policy. In this context, it may be useful to see coalitions as going through phases, in which they

(1) merely raise issues in the community;

(2) seek to get these issues on the formal agenda;

(3) attempt to get specific changes made; and

(4) focus on capturing the policy processes.

The phasing of goals and its connection to the concept of agenda-setting discussed in the literature illustrates the dynamic nature of strategy development (Nelson, 1984). Coalitions on a continual basis can readjust and prioritize goals in order to take into account the most effective courses of action. The dynamic nature of strategy is captured by the following definition:

Strategy is the science and art of mobilizing resources towards goals. It involves choice and sequence, staging and timing, and some combination of roles and styles. Strategy shows commitment to think ahead, anticipate alternatives, and achieve results. (Checkoway, 1987)

Strategies can also vary by level within the coalition. The grand strategy for the coalition may be to capture the policy process or to become the major source of ideas for change while the policy process is searching for solutions. At a less general level, intermediate and more specific strategies for raising money, hiring paid staff, drafting legislation, improving the image of the coalition in the community, or, as illustrated in the next chapter, engaging in a wide variety of nonpolitical cooperative efforts may be just as critical to the overall success of the coalition.

In sum, strategy development includes the selection of goals, the establishment of time frames, and the determination of broad, intermediate, and specific levels within the coalition for strategy development. Chapter 3 emphasized the use of an advocacy strategy committee within the coalition both to develop strategies and to monitor their implementation. It is recommended that strategy development and implementation should not be left haphazardly to a handful of leaders in the coalition.

Successful coalitions approach strategy development in a systematic and deliberate manner. Accordingly, a good practice guideline is that continual attention to strategic planning or the ongoing adjustment of means and ends within the coalition should be emphasized (Bryson, 1988). It is not enough to identify broad goals for the coalition; attention should be paid to intermediate and specific goals as well. Intermediate goals can be phased in and connected to and integrated with tactics, approaches, and style. In this respect, the leader or leadership group of a coalition should be encouraged to develop the ability to think conceptually and to be able to further the process of institutionalization of the organization (Katz, 1988).

Stop and Think

When was the last time that a coalition in which you participated systematically and comprehensively discussed and articulated its basic strategies? What mechanisms can you suggest to coalitions so that they can improve upon their development of strategies? If coalitions in which you have been a member have not discussed strategies, why was that the case? What are the barriers to more deliberate strategy development within coalitions?

IDENTIFYING COALITION RESOURCES

Coalitions have many resources available to them to help them achieve their goals. It is important for coalition leaders to keep in mind that it is wise for them to start with the resources of their own members before considering the use of resources of people and groups outside of the coalition. There are six major resources that most coalitions should examine for use on a regular basis. These are regularly identified in the growing body of literature on resource development (Lauffer, 1983; Pierce, 1984; Siporin, 1987):

(1) money

(2) energy or time

(3) facilities

(4) political legitimacy

(5) expertise and knowledge

(6) political mobilization

Money, of course, can be used as a substitute for some or all of the other resources listed above, since these resources can be purchased from individuals or groups. Every coalition can use liquid cash or easily convertible assets to purchase resources for the action plan. Because of the importance of money, coalitions should be encouraged to try to establish dues for members, to hold fund-raisers, and to seek external funding from foundations or other interested groups.

As one of the case studies in Chapter 2 reveals, a coalition that takes money from a government source faces the possibility of being co-opted by that source at some later time. As a result, caution should be exercised if a coalition is considering taking a government grant or contract. This type of fiscal relationship often entitles the government to muffle the advocacy effort when the coalition gets too close to upsetting the policies and programs of the current administration. Independent funding sources ensure independence in political action. Many of the coalitions discussed in Chapter 2 had minimal or no money at all, yet they were still successful in their advocacy efforts.

Energy, or *time,* is an abundant coalition resource. Most coalition members are expected to give of their time freely and to participate in the coalition regardless of their motivation. The cases in Chapter 2 confirm this willingness to participate. A majority of the coalitions discussed in this book have memberships that consist disproportionately of middle- or upper-middle-class professionals, agency personnel, or community residents. These types of coalition members freely give their time as long as the incentives for participation remain attractive. They do not expect to be compensated directly for their efforts.

The ethos of coalition members in the human services is that for the most part tangible rewards or compensation for coalition participation are not expected. The spirit of voluntarism remains strong. That is why many viable coalitions are able to operate without or with only minimal monetary resources as long as in-kind assistance is given to the coalition by its members. There are also added benefits when coalition members work in agencies: They can use the photocopiers in their workplaces for duplicating coalition materials, and they can use other agency equipment or resources for completing work needed by the coalition. Agency personnel may not only be released during working hours to participate in coalition activities, but their travel/lodging expenses are frequently paid by their employers. These resources can substitute for paid coalition staff.

Because coalition agendas may directly affect agencies' viability, many agencies struggle with the question of giving released time to their employees to participate in coalitions. The message here is that agencies should periodically assess the costs and benefits of coalition participation. The practice of granting released time for coalition participation is becoming more frequent, but it does raise the perennial Hatch Act question of whether employees or organizations receiving public funds can allow their employees to participate in political action through coalitions. One of the coalitions discussed in Chapter 2 even called itself an "association," so that the political nature of the group's activities would not be so obvious. This same coalition also carefully monitored its tactics so that the most covert political acts were avoided.

Facilities constitute still another resource for the coalition. Largely because many coalitions tend to be temporary in nature, with memberships often changing because of the nature of the issues coalitions work on, it is rare to find coalitions with permanent facilities in the form of office space or meeting rooms. For example, only one of the coalitions in Chapter 2 had permanent facilities or offices. Nevertheless, coalitions often find it quite easy to locate facilities that enable them to perform the tasks connected to coalition strategies. For example, coalitions can use churches, public buildings, agency boardrooms, and other community facilities to hold their meetings, strategy sessions, fundraisers, and cocktail parties. Because coalition members are frequently well connected in their communities, finding space for coalition business is usually not an issue.

Also, coalition leaders may keep coalition accounting ledgers, stationery, correspondence, and other materials in their homes, thus precluding the need for permanent office space. In the event a coalition wants to hire a paid lobbyist, the issue of permanent office space may become more critical. If a lobbyist is only part-time, office space may be unnecessary. If the lobbyist becomes full-time and is located in a state capital or large urban area, office space may become a necessity.

The issue of a permanent facility raises in a very concrete way the long-range direction of the coalition. If a coalition is temporary, it may settle for donated space, and the leaders will usually be content to work out of their homes or even take calls at their places of employment. However, as a coalition moves toward permanence by hiring paid staff and broadening its agenda and related activities, it will sooner or later have to deal with the possibility of a permanent location. The most important point is that the use of facilities is generally easy to obtain for the types of coalitions discussed in this book, because members of these coalitions have regular access to donated space for coalition activities.

Political legitimacy is also necessary for any successful coalition. Without political legitimacy, coalitions have limited access to decision makers in the policy processes. Political legitimacy comes from a variety of sources. It can come from the members of the coalition—who they are as individuals and whom they represent if they hold formal positions in their communities or agencies. Political legitimacy in this instance stems from members' perceived expertise or their association with respected professional organizations or human services agencies.

Additionally, decision makers may perceive a coalition as representing the interests of certain client groups. In this case, decision makers turn to the coalition for advice and solutions either because they feel the coalition is in the best position to understand these client groups or because they feel that the coalition directly represents the political interests of the client groups. In either case, the coalition has political legitimacy and can use it as part of its strategy to have an impact on the public policy process.

Finally, political legitimacy can come from members' access to other community resources. Coalition members may be able to tap money, energy, facilities, and expertise/knowledge, and to secure these resources for coalition use. Decision makers respect coalitions that can gain access to community resources because they realize that the coalitions will be able to use these resources to advocate for their interests

(Ornstein & Elder, 1978). Political legitimacy in this example is derived from the potential access of the coalition to other community resources.

Expertise and knowledge are also critical resources for coalitions. The memberships of coalitions often include lawyers, doctors, accountants, investors, researchers, and experienced agency or program directors. These individuals in their own right are experts in their communities, and their expertise may be accepted regardless of their participation in and affiliation with coalitions. When the case of a coalition is being presented, coalition members who are perceived of as experts are frequently called upon to present the positions of the coalition. Again, the idea is that decision makers will look beyond these persons' connections with the coalition and respect and value their opinions based on their known expertise and their reputations in the community. Coalitions often pursue individuals to join them because of their known expertise or their reputations.

Political mobilization is usually thought of as a tactic that lurks in the background. If friendly persuasion and other tactics do not work, then the coalition may consciously seek to mobilize its members to engage in direct political activity. The coalition may even decide to ask its members to contact friends and colleagues outside of the coalition to assist them in carrying out covert political activity. The ability of coalitions to mobilize their membership politically as well as to mobilize people outside the coalition sends shudders down the spines of many decision makers. The political efforts may be electoral in nature or they may involve direct lobbying, arm twisting, and the use of other political threats.

In this context, political mobilization may be thought of simultaneously as both a tactic and a resource. It is a resource because it can be turned to in the development of tactics—here mobilization is gaining access to resources. It is a tactic when there is a discussion of how these resources will be used.

It is critical that coalitions, by using advocacy strategy committees, annual retreats, and/or other mechanisms, assess on a regular basis what resources they have and what resources they will need to acquire in the near future. The skillful management of resources joins strategy development and implementation as an essential area for coalition leaders to focus on. Skillful management of resources, in turn, involves paying attention to both the task and interpersonal or relationship-oriented needs of groups (Friesen, 1987).

DIAGNOSING THE PUBLIC POLICY
ENVIRONMENT AND PROCESS

Effective strategy development also requires a good understanding of the operations of the different public policy environments and their processes. Public policy environments and their processes, for example, have formal as well as informal rules, follow different time cycles, have clearly defined and accepted communication patterns, and use consistent decision rules or criteria to make critical decisions (Dluhy, 1981b). There are three public policy environments that most coalitions will work in when they strive to achieve their political goals and objectives: legislative, bureaucratic, and fiscal.

As indicated earlier, Chapter 5 will focus more generally on the community environment and how coalitions go about achieving nonpolitical goals. Here, I concentrate on the achievement of political goals in the public policy environment. First, there is the *legislative* environment and process, which is dominated by elected officials and their professional staffs. This policy environment sets the broad framework for policies and programs and is responsible for adopting the annual appropriations needed to implement these policies and programs. Second, there is the *bureaucratic* environment and process, which includes the people responsible for monitoring the implementation of these policies and programs. This environment is mainly responsible for implementing the policies and programs established by the legislative environment. Key actors within government draft the rules of administration and oversee and periodically evaluate the policies and programs. The *fiscal* environment and process includes a narrower set of responsibilities. Other important government actors in this arena monitor the fiscal aspects of policies and programs. They audit the money spent and verify and legitimate expenditures for the program or service. Their job is to make sure that the money is being spent as was legally intended. The fiscal environment and process are not as interested in questions of impact or effectiveness of programs and services as they are in whether the programs and services are getting to the right people and that the procedures for spending money on these clients follow sound legal and accounting practices.

LEGISLATIVE ENVIRONMENT AND PROCESS

Although there are written rules of parliamentary procedure, many legislators follow unwritten rules when it comes to how they will make decisions and interact with lobbyists, coalitions, and the general public (Matthews, 1960). Legislators often prefer face-to-face interaction, and it is hard to separate their work environment from their social environment—some legislators are always doing business. For this reason, coalition members are encouraged to seek access to legislators through the more informal social network. Because many legislators are very willing to make deals "off the record," coalition members should not make promises that they may be unable to keep. Nevertheless, if there is a predominant unwritten norm, it is that reciprocity is honored (Oleszek, 1978). Legislators, like others, will engage in exchanges of things if they perceive these exchanges as mutually beneficial. Coalitions cannot just ask for favors, they must be prepared to deliver something of value to legislators in return (Dear & Patti, 1981; Dluhy, 1981a).

The time cycles of the legislative environment are well defined in constitutions and charters. Formal legislation and appropriations must be enacted during specified times. However, the legislative environment can respond to emergencies or crises by calling special sessions. In this sense, the process is flexible. Legislative cycles invariably follow the sequence of a rush to get things in, a lull, and then a great flurry near the end of the formal legislative cycle or the end of the fiscal year (Keefe & Ogul, 1977). The rush at the end reinforces informal bargaining and reciprocity, which are at the heart of this process.

Communication patterns in the legislative environment follow two predominant trends. Either communication is very formal and symbolic, as with prepared legislative testimony or formal press conferences, or it is informal, behind the scenes, and in person. In fact, one of the hallmarks of the legislative environment is the emphasis placed on personal communication and face-to-face lobbying (Ornstein & Elder, 1978). The predominant decision-making criteria used in the process are favoritism and political credit (Dexter, 1969). Those seeking favors from elected officials build up credit with them by nurturing them, delivering votes, giving them other political support, providing them with information from back home that is critical to their jobs, and so on. In short, reciprocity is a two-way street—those seeking favors must also deliver (Dluhy, 1981b).

The implications of this brief sketch of the legislative environment for strategy and tactics development are significant. Both my observations and much of the literature on legislative strategies support the following practice guidelines:

- Advance the careers of legislators whenever possible.
- Lobby legislators on a regular basis; do not show up only once a year.
- Do favors for legislators and build up credit.
- Get on the formal agenda early and stay there.
- Build your coalition of support ahead of time; do not wait until the last minute to assemble political support.
- Make your recommendations feasible or at least make them appear incremental, so that the change is not too threatening.
- Whenever possible, establish the principle first and then come back periodically to get the entire package piece by piece.
- Organize and communicate to legislators what their constituents are thinking and how these constituents are likely to react to your proposals.

BUREAUCRATIC ENVIRONMENT AND PROCESS

Bureaucracies take on lives of their own (Downs, 1967). Their survival interests dominate how they operate on a day-to-day basis. People working in bureaucracies often become loyal to the agencies and their survival, often losing sight of the programs and their mission. Because most bureaucracies are staffed by career civil servants, motivating these workers to support the interests of the coalition becomes a critical challenge for many coalitions. Since career civil servants are known to be very vulnerable to attacks from the media and the legislature, they often become very cautious in their behavior and are rarely willing to get too far out in front on an issue of importance to a coalition.

While rules and procedures are formal in most bureaucracies, and career employees hide behind them, on certain occasions bureaucrats will deviate from the rules when necessary. For example, time cycles are well defined, but extensions are frequently granted as long as requests for extensions are made through the appropriate channels. Communication patterns are usually very impersonal with strangers, but once credibility and identification with a social network are established, interaction patterns can often become very personal and informal (Bell & Bell, 1982; Seidman, 1970).

The principal criterion used within the bureaucratic environment and process for decision-making purposes is whether people, agencies, or coalitions are able to deliver—that is, prove that their programs work and that clients are being served. Bureaucrats frequently are focused on proving to their critics in the media and the legislature that their programs do work and that these programs deserve continued financial support (Carter, 1983). By implication, coalitions should show results, show that their programs or the ones they are advocating for work, and convince the bureaucrats that their programs are models in the sense that they demonstrate best practice in the field. Since bureaucrats are vulnerable to external attacks and are often locked into uninteresting and unchallenging jobs, coalitions can profit by recognizing the stagnant nature of many bureaucracies (Dluhy, 1981b).

There are a number of additional implications for strategy and tactic development within coalitions that can be derived from examining the literature on the bureaucratic environment and strategy. My experience and much of the literature supports the following practice guidelines:

- Keep things in writing; meet the deadlines.
- Stroke bureaucrats, make them feel relevant and useful.
- Build informal networks of friendships and personal relationships.
- Do not publicly embarrass bureaucrats.
- Give bureaucrats the information they need to lobby inside government.
- Help to build a body of knowledge to justify programs; develop the justifications for programs.
- Offer incremental changes that can be made each year to make programs better.

FISCAL ENVIRONMENT AND PROCESS

At the heart of the fiscal environment and process is the commitment on the part of some government employees to guard the purse strings (Wildavsky, 1988). The orientation is to make sure that appropriated money is spent legally and that monetary transactions follow the legal and other accounting procedures dictated by professional practice. In the fiscal process, there is less concern about the impact and effect of programs and more concern with whether the programs are getting to the intended clients and whether the delivery of the programs can be documented (Lyden & Miller, 1982). In short, the interest is more in auditing than in evaluation (Carter, 1983).

The rules of administration in the fiscal environment are usually rigid and formalized, and most communication is usually kept in writing. Impersonality and hierarchical channels of communication are dominant, and equity—that is, treating each client equally regardless of circumstances—is often dogmatically followed. Personal favors, building up of credit, and reciprocity are avoided most of the time, and government employees frequently hide behind the rules. The need for documentation and the following of rigid time schedules is usually enforced. For the government employee, there is a constant struggle and pressure to relax his or her nonpartisan and neutral approach to administration (Downs, 1967). In the fiscal process, networking and the development of informal and more personal relationships are largely eschewed (Lynch, 1979).

The implications for strategy and tactic development within the coalition are clear, given this description of the environment and process. My experience and much of the literature on the fiscal environment and strategy reinforces the following practice guidelines:

- Prove your case on paper; supply the data.
- Make your data valid and reliable, so their authenticity is not in question.
- Meet deadlines and keep things in writing.
- Learn technocratic terms and language and use them when interacting with government employees.
- Automate client records and files for programs so that information is easily accessible for auditing purposes.
- Recognize and reinforce employees' commitment to professionalism and impartiality; make interactions impersonal and stress professionalism.
- Keep coalition members who are too emotional or political away from fiscal employees.
- Follow the chain of command in communicating with fiscal employees.

CHOOSING A COALITION APPROACH

Over time, many coalitions adopt consistent and regularized ways of going about accomplishing their objectives. The methods they use for accomplishing objectives will be referred to here as the *approach*. One of the critical distinctions made about coalitional approaches in the interviews conducted for this book has to do with whether the approach can be characterized as *hard sell* or *soft sell*.

The hard sell is a straightforward but very threatening approach to political action. At the heart of this approach is the willingness to go public, to embarrass decision makers in front of their constituents, the media, or other audiences with whom they are symbolically associated. This might involve such actions as going to court, releasing critical inside information to the press, going over subordinates' heads with criticism, using intermediaries to apply pressure, and even threatening retaliation at the polls. In the short run this approach may be effective, but in the long run it works counter to the attempts to build bridges and develop friendships that characterize the essence of the soft sell.

With the soft sell, the intent is to be low key and to interact behind the scenes with those in the process. In this approach one uses persuasion, appeals to values, plays to the decision makers' sense of rationality, and, often, appeals to loyalty and friendship. Under no conditions would covert pressure be used with this approach. While these simple distinctions in approach are easy to recognize, coalitions often have considerable difficulty because of the desire to mix approaches without anticipating the consequences. A good practice guideline, drawn from my interviews with coalition members, is this: Use the soft sell whenever possible; use the hard sell only when all else fails. Members of coalitions often struggle with their choice of approach; however, the best context in which to debate coalition approach is in terms of long-range strategies versus short-range strategies. Coalitions striving toward permanence cannot afford to alienate decision makers repeatedly by using the hard sell, yet those same coalitions may lose their momentum if they do not occasionally flex their muscles and do so. The use of alternative approaches discussed within the coalition is, therefore, an effective way of making sure the coalition is committed to an ongoing discussion of the costs and benefits of different courses of action.

As will be discussed shortly, the approach used is also closely connected to how politically active the coalition wants to become and how this political activity corresponds to the coalition's desired image of itself in the community. The bottom line is that the hard sell is a forceful but costly approach to be used in the short term, while the soft sell is a low-key but successful approach over the long term. When coalitions decide to use an approach differently, they should carefully weigh the consequences of doing so. Coalitions that follow the practice guideline of discussing and weighing their approaches carefully are likely to be most effective.

DEVELOPING A COALITION STYLE

Many coalitions develop clear and identifiable styles of presentation. They express themselves through their language, their written documents, their face-to-face interactions, and their use of tactics. This style of presentation takes form slowly and is closely intertwined with the styles of the key leaders in the coalition. After a time, the identity of the coalition is often associated with a predominant style of presentation. Although coalitions make their cases in different ways, I have observed three styles of presentation to be fairly typical in the coalitions studied for this book. The literature also supports these observations (Dluhy, 1986; Tropman, 1987). The three styles are dramaturgy, scientific rationality, and political rationality.

Dramaturgy above all else appeals to the values, emotions, and ideological predispositions of decision makers. The concept of dramaturgy is widely used in the field of political psychology (Edelman, 1971). When a coalition is making its case, it comes across to decision makers in a certain way. Whether the style of presentation is planned or not, a coalition that dramatizes events, tells distressing stories about clients or social problems, uses inflammatory or consciousness-raising language, and oversimplifies its case is often labeled as a particular kind of coalition (Dluhy, 1986).

Charismatic leaders of coalitions are able consistently to capture the attention of decision makers by appealing to their sense of guilt or responsibility. This style is persuasive because of its action orientation, its clear-cut solutions, and its simplicity. Dramaturgy has little use for research, fact finding, or evaluation of the options. As one member of a successful coalition said in an interview:

> If decision makers can relate personally to the client or the problem being discussed, research and careful documentation of the problem are not necessary. Therefore, go right for their heart. Show them that they have sympathy for your cause. They will disregard all other arguments.

> **Stop and Think**
>
> How often have you stressed the sympathy factor?

Dramaturgy, therefore, stresses the value content of the argument. It assumes that decision makers are persuaded primarily by their identification with the client or the problem. Further, it assumes that decision makers want a simple, straightforward presentation of the case by the coalition. They may have little patience for research, analysis, and comparisons that might be made about the range of options available. This style, above all, stresses action. Coalitions using dramaturgy emphasize solutions and commitment, not complicated programs and policies. They often call for bold and innovative interventions that can be implemented within six months. Of course, not all decision makers are receptive to dramaturgy, but adroit coalition leaders should be able to identify decision makers who would be receptive to this style of presentation.

Scientific rationality constitutes a second style of presentation. At the base of this style is the appeal to an objective sense of rationality. The traditional problem-solving model represented in the community organization literature emphasizes this style (Cox, 1987). Using the problem-solving model, coalitions are guided by a sense of proving their position through the careful analysis of facts, the comprehensive examination of the options, and the unbiased selection of the solutions. Therefore, presentations would be very factual and statements would be documented and proved. Further, the manner of presenting facts would be to make assumptions and biases clear, the presentation as neutral in tone as possible, and the discussion of options exhaustive and comprehensive. Decision makers who are receptive to this style will often feel that they have been fully briefed and that they have gained both conceptual and theoretical orientations to the problem or client group (Dluhy, 1986). This style, while not dramatic, is persuasive because it is thorough, systematic, and, above all, factual. As one coalition member I interviewed said:

> You need to convince the decision makers that you are credible and professional and that you have the facts to back your case up with. If you can also convince them that there is no single option that you prefer, they

may rely on you for advice. Otherwise they will think your recommendations are self-serving.

Scientific rationality as a style of presentation is the one most frequently taught in graduate professional programs (Tropman, 1987). As
a result, coalition members with advanced professional degrees will
find this style familiar and easy to follow. However, as with the other
styles discussed in this chapter, only certain types of decision makers
will be receptive to this manner of presentation. The practice guideline
is to encourage coalition members and especially the leadership to
become skilled at identifying which style of presentation should be
used. This choice should be based on an examination of the audience to
which they will be presenting.

Political rationality is the third style of presentation. The essence of
this style is the appeal to feasibility and what will be most likely to pass
or be adopted. A common phrase used in discussions of political bargaining is "that which is feasible is that which is incremental or can be
made to appear incremental" (Dluhy, 1984). The focus on feasibility is
a common theme for many writers who analyze politics and decision
making, and they use this concept frequently (Lindblom, 1965; Wildavsky, 1988).

For this style to be effective, the coalition's case must be brief and to
the point. While data and research may be used in making the case, this
factual information is used mainly to legitimate a particular option or
recommendation (Rein, 1976). Only politically feasible options are
usually discussed.

When a small number of these feasible options are discussed, the
emphasis is on identifying the trade-offs among the options. The goal
is to have one implementable option be adopted. As a result, discussions
in this type of presentation focus less on consciousness raising (as in
dramaturgy) or exhaustive examinations of the problem and its solutions (as in the traditional problem-solving model). Rather, they focus
more on weighing the critical political factors that will lead to the
adoption of the option. Because this style is so pragmatic in orientation,
a frequent complaint that I have heard from coalition members is that
such heavy focus on what will go or what will be accepted may result
in the adopted options or solutions being largely marginal or incremental. Long-term or structural solutions to problems are eschewed in order
to make sure that incremental progress is made. One coalition member
who was interviewed appropriately said:

We always stress the next steps because we feel it is more important to make progress each year on our broad agenda than it is to reeducate decision makers toward the big picture.

I suggest that coalitions do two things before they adopt a dominant style of presentation. First, they should carefully assess the skills of the coalition members and the principal leaders to determine which style is the most natural to the group and which style the individual coalition members feel the most confident with. Second, and more important, they should look at the audiences they are trying to influence. What types of presentations will these audiences be receptive to? Can the coalition adapt its style to these different audiences? While it may not be good strategy to try out different styles continuously, it is a good idea to experiment a little with styles that fit audiences that the coalition is trying to influence. Over time, many coalitions will become known for their particular styles of presentation. An image based on a predominant style can easily evolve over time because of the experiences and interactions between the coalition and various decision-making bodies.

Stop and Think

Can you identify the dominant style in each coalition that you have been a member of? Has this style changed recently in any of these coalitions? Why?

SELECTING COALITION TACTICS

Tactics are the tools used by coalitions for goal achievement. Without a plan of action, strategies, an approach, and a predominant style of presentation as guides for action, tactics cannot be appropriately selected and used. One of the main jobs of leadership within the coalition is to select tactics that are directed strategically toward the main goals of the coalition. This important link between goals and tactics is emphasized by many organizational theorists (Sarri, 1987; Selznick, 1957).

As noted earlier, one of the frequent complaints of coalition members is that they have been asked to do things that are not connected effectively to a plan of action for the coalition. The practice guideline here is that coalition members cannot afford to waste time, because

coalition membership is usually not their primary organizational affiliation or their primary personal concern (Olson, 1968). Therefore, it is
very helpful if active participation in the coalition is aimed at purpose-
ful activity.

Following are some of the more frequently used tactics identified in
the interviews with coalition members. These are isolated here to
provide a wide range of tactics to look at when making a pragmatic
selection of activities for the members of a coalition. Many of these
tactics have also been discussed and illustrated in the literature on
political action (Alexander, 1982; Sharwell, 1982; Thursz, 1971).

(1) The legislative day. A common activity is to bring the coalition
members and even clients together for a "legislative day." The activity
takes place most frequently in Washington, D.C., or state capitals,
although this activity is now being used more frequently with city
councils and county commissions as well. The basic activity is to bring
the entire membership of the coalition together for a day. At different
points during the day, elective officials may be invited to address the
group on key issues. For the rest of the day, coalition members can make
personal visits to key legislators' offices for private conversations and
face-to-face lobbying. A press conference is often part of the day, and
usually a social hour in the evening, to which legislators are invited, is
a popular way to finish the event. Some coalitions present their entire
legislative agenda for the year at such an event, or they may present a
specific piece of legislation or a proposal that they wish to publicize.
The legislative day is a morale booster for coalition members and a
publicity tactic for gaining coalition visibility. The face-to-face lobbying conducted during the day may also be productive. These events
require considerable advanced planning and a significant use of coalition resources. Thus these kinds of events should be carefully examined
before they are used.

(2) Face-to-face lobbying. This is a common tactic used by many
coalition members. If the members have easy access to elected officials
and the state capital or city hall is not too distant, then this tactic is
almost always preferred. Legislative days, as illustrated above, are
often a substitute for face-to-face lobbying because coalition members
are too far from the capital to be engaged in this kind of lobbying on a
regular basis. Many of the coalition members interviewed felt that
direct lobbying by their membership is far superior to lobbying done by
paid lobbyists. While they indicated that legislators are used to professional lobbyists and their manner of persuasion, they also pointed out

that legislators welcome feedback from back home in the form of direct input about clients and problems. In the long run, this direct input often helps legislators to understand and make their case more effectively with their peers in the legislative branch.

(3) Indirect communication and communication through intermediaries. Another common tactic mentioned was the use of letter writing and telegrams to influence the public policy process. If a campaign can generate large numbers of letters, telegrams, and telephone calls, its message can be dramatically communicated in a short period of time. While decision makers often know that these communications are part of a campaign, separate and individual communications—as opposed to petitions or form letters—are usually more effective as a tactic. Coalition members can ask colleagues at work, who may not be in the coalition, or they can ask board members or highly influential friends in the community to contact decision makers on behalf of the coalition issues.

The key to using this tactic, according to the interviews, is assuring that each communication is seen as personal and that the individual making the contact is communicating his or her own wishes. In short, the individual should strive to demonstrate that he or she has gone to some effort to expend time to make his or her views known. This demonstrates to the decision maker that the coalition members' efforts consumed more time than just signing a petition or sending a form letter. Legislators are frequently known to look for emotional and political intensity on the part of people who seek to influence them.

(4) Expert testimony. Coalitions are also called upon to deliver expert testimony. An important aspect of giving this testimony is conveying competence and establishing credibility. It is very helpful if legislators feel that the coalition's testimony is believable and accurate and represents a coherent solution to the problem. Legislators are known to seek statements for the record. Many of them want to know where organizations stand. At the same time, they also seek expert advice, especially during question-and-answer periods. When coalitions are viewed as experts, their credibility is rarely questioned.

Coalition members interviewed have found that it is helpful to rehearse their presentations, and they have also found it useful to select presenters carefully. A standard format is one in which the coalition submits a formal written statement to a legislative committee and then follows this with highlights or a paraphrasing of the statement for the legislators. The presentation is usually followed by open discussion. It is recommended that written statements be concise and well written. These statements are taken seriously and they are for the record. The oral presentation supplements the written statement, and a good practice guideline is that this presentation should primarily be directed at establishing the coalition's credibility and integrity.

(5) Program or service justification statement. Another common tactic is to develop a written statement that justifies the need for a program or service for which a coalition is advocating. This statement is often widely distributed and discussed. There are three fundamental parts that are useful to cover in this statement. First, the coalition tries to prove that there is a demonstrated need for the program in the community. This involves using data to establish unmet need, identification of the benefits that will be achieved by these types of programs or services, and proving that no other existing programs or services in the community currently meet the perceived needs. Second, the coalition attempts to demonstrate why the members of the coalition are in the best position to design the delivery system that will be used to implement the program or service. The coalition does more than just advocate for the program or service; it also offers a design for implementation. Third, it is helpful to show that this program or service will be cost-effective, that is, that the objectives can be realized in a cost-effective way using the design recommended by the coalition. This tactic is useful for decision makers who want succinct, written justifications for programs or services they are being asked to fund or adopt for the first time.

(6) Needs assessment. I was told in many of the interviews that coalitions are increasingly turning to formal research studies in the form of needs assessments to use as they advocate for change. The art and science of doing needs assessments has improved substantially, and government agencies, foundations, and other external funding bodies are very willing to fund needs assessments before new investments of resources are made.

While needs assessment formats vary considerably, they are basically applied research studies that document community or client problems, specify unmet needs, and evaluate the most feasible solutions to the problem. These assessments are usually conducted by applied researchers who are not members of the coalition. Good needs assessments should be able to stand up to professional scrutiny from the research community. This tactic, while useful, can be expensive and can take a considerable amount of time to complete. It is clearly a long-range tactic, since it may take five or six months at a minimum to complete such a study.

(7) Position papers. Another more recently used tactic is to produce a position paper for the coalition. According to the interviews, the position paper is longer and more elaborate than the type of statement that would be given during expert testimony. It has also been described as conceptually broader than a program or service justification statement. The major purpose of the position paper is to develop a political, economic, and social rationale for change.

The position paper identifies the problem, looks at options for solving it, and carefully weighs alternative solutions. It is not a research exercise, like the needs assessment; rather, it is a sound analytical exercise that develops the justification for action. A specific version of the position paper is the position statement, which is a brief reaction to specific legislation or resolutions that are pending before legislative bodies. The statement delineates the reaction to the legislation and then gives a brief rationale for this position.

(8) Campaign work. One of the most controversial tactics identified during the interviews was the involvement of coalition members in the campaigns of elected officials. While coalition members participate as private citizens, it is usually clear that they also represent the interests of their agencies or their professions. Campaign work may involve fund-raising, volunteering to take part in campaign activities, or writing speeches or position statements. Coalition members may also be called upon to contact colleagues, agency board members, and friends in the community to work in the campaign. By soliciting support for candidates from these people, coalition members may draw themselves more deeply into partisan political campaigns. Nevertheless, many politically savvy coalition members interviewed for this book consistently participated in legislative campaigns and reported that this participation often gave them and their coalitions direct and immediate access to elected officials to make their case.

(9) Protest. Although it has become unfashionable to talk about nonviolent protest as a tactic, it nevertheless may be the only option under certain circumstances. Sit-ins, picketing, and economic boycotts are used less frequently today than they were in the 1960s, but the threat of protest always looms behind the scene. Violent protest is not acceptable today when using conventional tactics.

(10) Keeping the channels of communication open. One of the tactics for coalition members identified frequently in the interviews was

building up personal and professional relationships with decision makers within the public policy environment. These relationships may be nurtured through purely social meetings, visits, cocktail parties, dining engagements, invitations to decision makers to visit and speak to the coalition, or various other contacts that are low key and not necessarily aimed at dealing with anything specific. These contacts may be more social than political, even though, in the long run, access may be established as a result of these social encounters.

Coalition leaders, in particular, report that they spend a lot of time building networks of support among decision makers in the public policy environment so that when specific action is necessary, the preliminary social interactions that build trust and confidence can be skipped. If there is an overall practice guideline derived from the interviews with coalition members, it is that coalitions should regularly keep decision makers informed of coalition activities through newsletters, visits, and other written materials. Coalitions can also periodically invite decision makers to visit their communities and to attend coalition meetings or visit agencies or programs of coalition members.

Many savvy coalition members interviewed indicated that is it wise to "give a decision maker, particularly a legislator, an annual award for distinguished service or accomplishments." This shows the appreciation of the coalition for the legislator's support.

In Chapter 3, I recommended that coalitions periodically survey their memberships to determine which activities (tactics) members would be willing to engage in. The leadership and/or advocacy strategy committee could then make appropriate assignments based on members' expertise as well as their willingness to perform these activities. The main strategic concern is that tactics should be selected carefully and that this selection should follow the overall plan of action so that the coalition members do not waste valuable time.

One additional suggestion is to examine the tactics presented in this section in terms of how they correspond to the style of presentation that a coalition may be using. For example, the tactics can be grouped according to whether they fit comfortably into each of the three styles of presentation presented earlier in this chapter. Consider these as practice guidelines:

- *Dramaturgy:* Use the legislative day, face-to-face lobbying, expert testimony, the position paper, campaign work, protest, and keeping the channels of communication open.

- *Scientific rationality:* Use expert testimony, the program or service justification statement, the needs assessment, and the position paper.
- *Political rationality:* Use the legislative day, face-to-face lobbying, communication through intermediaries, the position paper, campaign work, and keeping the channels of communication open.

POLITICAL ACTIVISM VERSUS
PROFESSIONAL NEUTRALITY

Neutral professional postures are often inbred in social work and other types of direct service professions (Dluhy, 1984). As a result, many coalitions that have large numbers of professionally trained individuals as their members may encounter difficulties with the problem of "dirty hands." The boundaries of political activity are often difficult to draw in coalitions and other kinds of groups dominated by professionals (Walzer, 1973). While most of the coalition members interviewed indicated that their members were willing to get their hands a "little dirty" in politics, few wanted major and intensive political involvement.

Practitioners may view their role as one of clarifying options rather than of taking positions, for fear that association with a narrow or focused point of view may limit their effectiveness in other areas or around other issues. According to many of the interviews, professionals are sometimes characterized by this tendency to want to keep from getting their hands dirty. For example, it was reported that some of the members of the coalitions studied had little resistance to making telephone calls to legislators, occasionally making personal visits to the offices of legislators or bureaucrats, writing letters or sending telegrams to public officials, or giving expert testimony. Resistance surfaced, however, when members were asked to campaign for political candidates, contribute money to political campaigns, hold fund-raisers for candidates, or give candidates the names, addresses, and telephone numbers of their board members so that they could be contacted for political purposes. The dilemma of where to draw the line in political activity is common within coalitions and other groups having professionals as members (Wolk, 1981). It is too easy simply to argue that the end justifies the means.

Since professionals are touchy about their image, a reasonable solution to this dilemma may be to have the coalition openly and freely discuss the issue, debate it, and, where necessary, develop a policy for the entire group. Often members may endorse certain political tactics as long as they are not asked to be involved in such activities themselves. Other times, as portrayed in the case studies, members may wish to leave the coalition if it becomes too political. In the end, a coalition, because of its fundamental political purpose, will have to find ways for professional concerns and images to coexist with the need for activity aimed at furthering the major political goals of the coalition. Once a coalition enters the political arena, the problem of "dirty hands" is unavoidable.

SUMMARY: DEVELOPING A PLAN OF ACTION

Chapter 3 examined how to organize and then maintain a coalition. The focus was on organizational development and the stages that coalitions go through as they become institutionalized. This chapter has dealt primarily with the elements that must be considered in order to develop a comprehensive plan of action for the coalition. The development of the plan constitutes another critical phase of organizational development. In this context, coalitions should consider the following practice guidelines:

- Make sure that the strategies, or the ways in which means and ends are connected, are clear to the members of the coalition.
- Develop a way to identify the resources or the tangible and intangible things that will need to be used to make the coalition operate effectively on a day-to-day basis.
- Examine carefully the norms of the public policy environment and processes the coalition will be working in.
- Clarify the major approach or method to be used by the coalition to implement its strategies.
- Choose carefully the style of presentation or the way in which the coalition will make its case to decision makers.
- Evaluate the tactics or activities that coalition members can get involved in and make sure they are connected to the overall plan.

Most important, coalitions that develop an orientation toward periodic assessment of these practices will be in the best position to plan for the future. A plan of action that covers the major points raised in this chapter is a good starting point. This plan of action can always be modified or changed, but without such a plan, a coalition may easily become ineffectual and disband.

EXERCISE FOR PRACTITIONERS

Read the following statement, which describes one of the members of a coalition advocating for runaway youth in a community.

The Sunshine House provides temporary short-term care, shelter, and counseling for homeless youth and their families. We believe that homeless youth are a responsibility of the community. Whenever possible, we try to help families achieve reconciliation without sacrificing the individual's capacity for self-determination. We have always believed in having people help themselves. We operate a 24-hour crisis hot line, maintain a network of foster homes that can provide temporary shelter for young people, provide counseling and information and referral services, sponsor parents' support groups, and run a community outreach program in the public schools, community agencies, and local media. No other organization in our community offers the breadth or depth of services that we do. Since we are staffed primarily by volunteers, we are able to offer all of these services at reduced cost. For example, comparative figures collected by the Department of Social Services show that we have a per hour client cost of $2.53, while the average per hour client cost is $5.23 for a sample of 50 agencies in our community. Our management practices also keep costs down—particularly because of our participation in a food co-op. Nowhere else in our community can homeless youth receive competent care at such a low cost.

Homeless youth, by our definition, are throwaways who have been ejected from their own homes, young people who are away from home by mutual agreement with their parents, and youth who are homeless for any other reason. Last year, we served 250 homeless youth in our community. The county sheriff and juvenile court also indicated that last year there were 650 reports of runaways. Since 90% of the youth we serve come from our own community, we feel we are doing a good job of serving the larger community needs. Since our program has been in existence (1985), the figures for teenage larceny have decreased by 10% and the incidence of drunk driving among minors has dropped by 12%.

We run a tight organization that is headed by three professionally trained clinicians with extensive training who train and supervise 15 volunteers. Periodic staff meetings and careful case management allow us to serve youth effectively. The best testimony to our program is in the fact that three former homeless youth served by our program are now members of our volunteer staff as well as full-time employees in three settings in our community.

First, in a group discussion, critique this statement, especially as it affects the image of one of the coalition members (programs). What are the strengths of the image portrayed in this statement? The weaknesses? How could this statement be improved? The idea is to change the statement so that decision makers and other members of the community will find the program attractive and credible, and therefore will view the coalition that represents these types of programs more favorably.

Second, consider and write down in outline form what your major strategies, approach, style, and tactics are likely to be for a coalition that includes members who run or who are supportive of programs like these. Take a step back and consider what a plan of action might look like for a coalition representing these kinds of programs and interests. In a group discussion, compare your plans of action.

Chapter 5

ACHIEVING NONPOLITICAL GOALS IN THE COMMUNITY

Even though the primary emphasis in coalitions is on achieving the political goal of having a successful impact on the public policy process, coalitions also engage in a wide variety of activities that are aimed at such nonpolitical goals as educating the community about critical social issues, generating nongovernment resources, improving service coordination and service delivery through cooperative efforts, sharing resources among organizations, and facilitating agency and program mergers. When a coalition is developing its plan of action, it is therefore wise for it to identify both political and nonpolitical goals.

Chapter 4 focused mainly on the achievement of political goals by successfully affecting the legislative, bureaucratic, and fiscal decision-making processes that are an integral part of the larger public policy environment. This chapter, in contrast, will focus on the community environment and the achievement of nonpolitical goals. As Chapter 4 pointed out, when putting together a plan of action, coalitions need to take into account the phasing and blending of different kinds of goals. For example, the most general goal of a coalition may be to exert influence successfully over the public policy process, but in order to do this, a coalition may need initially to establish and then enhance its credibility and legitimacy in the community.

In turn, this credibility and legitimacy may be increased by improving upon a whole range of voluntary and nonpolitical interactions that take place among organizations within (and outside) the coalition. Thus cooperative interaction among organizations in the nonpolitical arena can set the stage for more cooperative interaction in the political arena. The literature on organizational theory has documented extensively the importance of interorganizational cooperation and exchanges at the community level (for example, see Hasenfeld, 1983; Holland & Petchers, 1987; Levine & White, 1961).

Of particular interest in organizational theory is the concept of the task environment. This refers to a specific set of organizations and groups with which an organization exchanges resources and services and with whom this organization establishes specific modes of interaction (Hasenfeld, 1983). Interaction may be both cooperative and competitive, but in this chapter we focus only on cooperative interaction among organizations, because cooperation in the nonpolitical arena has a direct impact on the ability of organizations to cooperate on the achievement of goals in the political arena.

Past studies of administrators of human services agencies have shown that leaders of organizations are more likely to spend time on activities related to organizational maintenance and control functions than on goal attainment, especially the attainment of goals aimed at innovation, procuring additional resources, and planning for the future (Cyert, 1975; Patti, 1983). Thus one important challenge to organizations and their leaders is to join coalitions. Coalitions, in turn, can provide these organizations with both political and nonpolitical benefits that they could not secure if their organizations acted alone. It is reasonable to argue that participation in coalitions will broaden the horizons of many administrators and move them in the direction of focusing on goal attainment and other activities aimed at adapting their organizations to a changing external environment. This will shift many administrators away from a predominant focus on the internal management of their organizations. The field of interorganizational relations, especially voluntary and cooperative exchanges through coalitions, is a growing area of interest within the broader field of organizational theory (Holland & Petchers, 1987).

Coalitions can take advantage of these nonpolitical modes of interaction to achieve other worthwhile goals. For leaders of organizations who are outcome rather than process oriented, this area of interaction offers another opportunity for them to achieve desirable and often very tangible results through joint action (Garner, 1989). The ability of a coalition to engage successfully in activity aimed at both political and nonpolitical goals illustrates the last major phase of organizational development for coalitions discussed in this book. When a coalition is able to achieve both types of goals, develop a plan of action, adapt itself over time to a changing task environment, and take on a more structured internal order, then it has transformed itself into an institution with considerable permanence (Selznick, 1957).

DIAGNOSING THE COMMUNITY ENVIRONMENT

Every organization has a task environment in the community to which it can relate. This environment can be very predictable and easy to negotiate for an individual organization, or it may be very complex and difficult to negotiate. Since most organization leaders will attempt to develop exchange linkages that benefit their organizations directly, there are many possibilities for collaboration within the community. Many of these exchange partners will come from coalitions, and therefore participation in coalitions offers an organization the opportunity to establish a wide variety of relationships that meet its nonpolitical goals. As a result, it is helpful for a coalition to diagnose the kind of task environment that exists in the community so that coalition members can engage in activities that achieve nonpolitical goals. Task environments can be described in different ways for the purposes of understanding the types of collaboration that are possible. There are four important characteristics of task environments that affect collaboration patterns (Hasenfeld, 1983): stability/instability, concentration and dispersion of resources, the extent of community resources, and homogeneity/heterogeneity of service technologies.

Stability/instability. The task environment may be experiencing the influx of new organizations, the termination of some existing organizations, or the change in mission of some already-existing organizations. In short, the environment may be highly unstable and changing or it may be stable and relatively predictable. From the standpoint of collaboration, a highly unstable environment means that organizations will often find coalitions very useful, since they allow the organizations to join groups and find partners for collaboration purposes. In this sense, an organization can be more efficient in scanning its environment because membership in a coalition will serve two purposes—it will allow the organization to be involved in joint political action as well as to make contacts and pursue nonpolitical collaboration. Under these circumstances, instability and uncertainty in the environment provide a number of incentives for an organization to join a coalition.

Alternatively, stable and predictable environments can be characterized by the already-established patterns of interaction. There is little incentive under these circumstances to join a coalition unless the current patterns of nonpolitical collaboration are judged as undesirable or there is a profound political issue. There are, in short, few incentives to join a coalition in a stable environment. The direct implication is that it will be more difficult to develop coalitions in stable environments and easier in unstable ones. Beyond this, coalition leadership will have to find very appealing political and nonpolitical issues for the coalition to work on in a stable environment because organizations will not necessarily be looking for new collaboration patterns or new partners to form coalitions with. In contrast, in unstable environments, getting the organizations together and establishing an ongoing coalitional structure will be more important. Thus leaders of coalitions in stable environments will find it very useful to have skills in issue framing, agenda-setting, and conflict management, while leaders of coalitions in unstable environments will find it very useful to have organizational development skills.

Concentration and dispersion of resources. Another characteristic of a task environment is the extent to which resources are concentrated within a few large, powerful organizations, dispersed relatively equally across organizations, or distributed in some mixed pattern. The distribution of resources is critical to the activity of coalitions. For example, if the task environment is characterized by a large number of relatively small organizations and these organizations have few resources, then there are clear incentives for these organizations to band together to achieve a variety of both political and nonpolitical goals. Collective action will often be superior to individual action, and, since no single organization has sufficient resources to act on its own, collaboration allows resource sharing.

Conversely, if the task environment is dominated by a handful of large and resource-rich organizations, while the remaining organizations are small and resource-poor, the large organizations will usually try to make it on their own and thus secure all the payoffs. The major interest in coalition participation usually comes from the small, resource-poor organizations banding together to take on the larger and more powerful organizations. The practice guideline illustrated here is that coalitions are more likely to be appealing to the weak than they are to the stronger organizations. There is usually a tendency for large, resource-rich organizations to try to do it on their own, without collaborative action, and an equally likely tendency for small, resource-poor organizations to band together so that their collective strength can be used.

Extent of community resources. Some communities have few resources available for the human services; they may have histories of not raising many funds for charity, and they may be politically unwilling to allocate many of their public tax dollars for human services. Under these circumstances, there are few resources available and a lot of competition for those resources. Here coalitions are needed to develop plans for allocating scarce resources, since if each organization goes its own way, there will be only a few resources available for a limited number of organizations. Collective action through a coalition offers a chance to guarantee some equity in resource distribution across the organizations in the coalition. Alternatively, some communities may have relatively generous resources available for the human services; they may have histories of raising substantial funds for charity, and they may have taxed themselves at high levels to pay for human services. Under these circumstances, there may be enough resources to go around (in a relative sense) and therefore organizations will find it easier to secure their own resources from a resource-rich environment. Thus collaboration through a coalition may be less attractive when there are more resources available in the community but more attractive when the overall environment is resource-poor.

Homogeneity/heterogeneity of service technologies. Each human service organization has a dominant service technology or a set of institutionalized procedures aimed at changing the physical, psychological, social, or cultural attributes of people in order to transform them from a given status to a new prescribed status (Hasenfeld, 1983). If the task environment is very complex and there is wide variation in the use of different service technologies, then organizations will be in direct competition for clients. Under these circumstances, coalitions would generally be avoided, since organizations would be in direct competition with one another for clients. Alternatively, if there is widespread use of only a few service technologies, then organizations would be more likely to cooperate by sharing clients, because they would have no major philosophical differences in the way they conducted their business or in what needed to be delivered to clients in the community. Coalitions could then cooperate, share clients by making referrals, and engage in other political activities that would enhance their mutual interests. In short, homogeneity of service technologies makes collaboration through coalitions more feasible, while heterogeneity of service technologies fosters competition and makes coalition building more difficult. This line of reasoning applies to the achievement of both political and nonpolitical goals.

Taking the above four characteristics of task environments into account, a number of summary observations are worth emphasizing; these may be viewed as practice guidelines. First, where task environments are unstable, resources are dispersed, resources are limited, and there are only a few service technologies, coalitions are more likely to form. Second and alternatively, where task environments are stable, resources are concentrated, resources are more abundant, and there are many and different service technologies present, coalitions are less likely to form because organizations are more likely to pursue their own interests independently. Third, given the importance of the task environment, the leaders within a coalition will find it helpful to recognize the characteristics of the task environment and the nature of interorganizational relationships so that they can develop a better plan of action (Sarri, 1987). When the conditions are not conducive to the formation of coalitions, the leaders will have to work extraordinarily hard to identify critical issues, both political and nonpolitical, that will make their coalition attractive to organizations that otherwise would not have many incentives to come together and form a coalition. Here issue development would be the priority for the leadership within the coalition. In contrast, where the conditions are ripe for coalition formation, such issues are more likely to emerge after the coalition has been developed. The priority for leadership under these conditions would be organizational development rather than issue development.

The clear message offered in this section is that where conditions are antithetical to coalition formation in the community, the overall strategy should be to emphasize issue development in the coalition; where the conditions are supportive of coalition formation, the overall strategy should be to emphasize organizational development.

SELECTING STRATEGIES AND TACTICS

Because coalitions have only limited resources and because members may have different reasons for joining, coalitions may have to choose between political and nonpolitical goals and find a workable balance between the two. For example, individual coalition members may find it very attractive to work in a task group that is writing a proposal to a foundation that may result in a grant to set up a computerized information and referral system. This activity would be aimed at the nonpolitical goal of improving service delivery in the community through more efficient client assessment and placement. However, at the same time, the same members may be asked to be involved in lobbying in the state capital for legislative changes that would make it mandatory for licensed social workers to have advanced degrees and substantial practice experience.

Which activity is the member more likely to participate in? The first activity is aimed at a nonpolitical goal, while the second is aimed at a political goal. Of course, there is no clear answer to this question, except that it would be nice if the member could do both. Nevertheless, one of the themes of this book is that coalitions should be more deliberative and assessment oriented, and the reassessment of strategies and tactics and the revision of the plan of action should be an ongoing task.

In practice, it is conceivable that much of the time spent by coalition members may be spent on collaborative activity aimed at achieving nonpolitical goals, with only small amounts of time being spent on activity aimed at achieving political goals. One of the critical tasks of leadership is to make sure that there are sufficient incentives to sustain coalition participation. Therefore, in selecting strategies and tactics, it would be useful if the leadership of the coalition would regularly turn to its membership for information and feedback so that the amount of time spent on activity that is aimed at the various goals of the coalition can be determined. Accordingly, I offer the following practice guidelines, which emerged during the interviews with coalition members:

- Complete regular surveys of the coalition membership to determine the tasks or activities in which members are willing to participate.
- Regularly poll coalition members concerning which nonpolitical goals and activities they think the coalition should be emphasizing.
- Have at least one political goal that the coalition is working on at all times, so the coalition does not lose it sense of political purpose.
- Use retreats and other intensive planning sessions periodically to readjust the coalition's plan of action.

Make sure the membership does not get burned out on activity that is aimed at achieving political goals. Especially when political activity is not successful, enthusiasm for the coalition can be revived by turning to activity that is nonpolitical in nature, but that may have more tangible payoffs for the members. The message is, when the coalition fails at politics, turn to constructive nonpolitical collaboration and resource sharing.

CITIZEN EDUCATION

Organizations that are members of a coalition may seek to work together on a regular basis to inform and educate the community about social issues and problems, especially ones that are directly connected to the organizations and their clients. In this way, the coalition establishes credibility and visibility on an issue. In a sense, the coalition may become the expert in the eyes of the community, and the community may turn to the coalition at a later date for advice when serious problem-solving begins. The first step is to educate the community about the issue or problem, but the next step is very likely to be defining and setting the political agenda (Nelson, 1984).

One common approach to informing and educating the community about an issue or problem is to have the coalition initiate or actually complete a study of the issue or problem in the community. Thus the organizations in the coalition may agree jointly to document a critical community problem by commissioning an evaluation study, a needs assessment, a cost-benefit analysis, or some other form of analysis (Dluhy et al., 1988; Siegel et al., 1987). The key point about studying the issue or problem is that whatever mechanism is used to document the problem, the coalition and its members should consider becoming visible proponents of this study and should consider participating in the study if that is feasible. In this way, the coalition pursues a nonpolitical goal, educating the community, that may prove to be beneficial to the credibility of each organization within the coalition as well as to the coalition as a whole. The coalition may get involved in a variety of ways, ranging from exerting pressure to make sure a study is done, to helping to prepare a grant application to get a study funded, to actually participating in the completion of the study or assisting in the dissemination of the study results. As discussed earlier, many members of a coalition who eschew more political involvement may be comfortable participating in tasks associated with documentation of community issues or problems.

Another way in which a coalition and its members can inform and educate the general public is through involvement in community forums (Siegel et al., 1987). Open discussion of community issues or problems is one of the initial steps in agenda-setting. Coalition members may advocate for these forums, actually organize the forums, or just participate in them. In any respect, the coalition will find it advantageous to be closely identified with forums that are aimed at educating and informing the community about issues and problems. In recent years, forums on homelessness, AIDS, and child abuse and neglect have been popular in most urban communities. Again, these activities are largely nonpolitical in nature in the beginning; however, later on, these activities may have a more clearly designated political purpose.

Members of the coalition can participate in these forums and establish new linkages with other groups and organizations in the community that may have a payoff at a later time when more political networking may be necessary. Therefore, besides educating the public, forums are also places where social networking occurs. Social networking may provide a secondary benefit for many members.

Closely related to forums are jointly sponsored conferences and workshops that are aimed specifically at professionals and service providers. These events are informative and not necessarily political. They may even be viewed as in-service training by some organizations. Collaboration around these events strengthens community ties and, as pointed out above, provides an immediate opportunity for social networking as well as a more long-range opportunity for political networking.

NONGOVERNMENT RESOURCE ACQUISITION

Although it is natural to look to government for more financial support for many human services, increasingly foundations, the voluntary sector, the private sector, and individual donors are also being turned to as sources of support (Lauffer, 1983). Additionally, while it may be advantageous for an individual organization to seek its own funding in order to maintain or expand programs or to develop new programs, there are many circumstances in which joint action or a partnership among organizations may be more desirable. In fact, nongovernment funding sources have frequently encouraged proposals submitted by groups of organizations in the community (Robert Wood Johnson Foundation, 1985).

There are many worthwhile projects that can be funded in communities where organizations are linked through partnerships (Lauffer, 1983). For example, there are numerous types of community education and dissemination projects, information and referral programs, cooperative training and staff development programs, and other networking projects in which the essence (goal) of the project or program is improved interaction among the organizations and service providers in the community. There are also many circumstances in which an application for funding is substantially enhanced by having a group of organizations as the applicant. As discussed in this chapter, organizations that are able to collaborate successfully in nonpolitical arenas, as in seeking nongovernment resources, will find it easier to collaborate in political arenas when the occasion occurs.

The case studies in Chapter 2 illustrate that some coalitions initially meet around a community issue or problem. These initial meetings may be aimed mainly at identifying a communitywide problem that is caused, at least in part, by the failure of the organizations and agencies in the community to cooperate and coordinate their activities successfully. As a result of these meetings, a coalition may adopt at the outset a nonpolitical goal, such as seeking nongovernment funding for a community-based coordination program or some other type of program that requires interorganizational cooperation. In fragmented and competitive service delivery environments, there are a lot of projects that can be developed to overcome the problems in access that clients experience because of their lack of knowledge of the system and their inability to qualify successfully for programs and services that have complicated eligibility rules and procedures.

From the interviews, there are a number of questions that members of an individual organization should ask themselves when they are contemplating a joint application for funding for a new program with other organizations in the community:

(1) Has the funding source designated that joint applications are either preferred or required?

(2) Will our organization receive a clear set of tangible benefits if this application is funded?

(3) Will joint action make the development of the proposal (application) easier because of the shared resources and expertise? This assumes that no single or individual organization has the time and resources to develop the proposal on its own.

(4) Will the joint application enhance the probability of the application being funded?

(5) Can this successful partnership between organizations easily spill over into other areas of cooperation at a later date?

Stop and Think

When is the last time you did an inventory of which activities in your organization could be enhanced by joint action and collaboration with other organizations in your task environment? Do you regularly assess the possibilities for joint funding applications, or do you just assume that unilateral action is most desirable?

In sum, collaboration by organizations that seek nongovernment resources is a common strategy that can be used by organizations. The case studies illustrate that some coalitions may form initially to achieve nonpolitical goals and then, at a later date, may use the positive experience in the partnership to enhance their ability to cooperate in achieving political goals. Projects that are specifically aimed at improving cooperation and coordination in the community among organizations and service providers are prime examples of the kinds of projects for which joint funding applications for new programs are possible.

INTERAGENCY COOPERATION AND COORDINATION

In addition to joint funding applications, organizations may find it beneficial to pursue a wide variety of other nonpolitical goals collaboratively. Again, this activity will reinforce and strengthen the ability of these organizations to work together when the objective is achieving more political goals. For example, collaborative planning and coordinating bodies are nonthreatening ways for organizations to meet regularly and discuss communitywide problems and issues. Information sharing and social networking may be the sole purpose of these kinds of meetings, or they can become the precursor for the development of a coalition with more immediate political goals.

On the other hand, organizations may want to establish contractual relationships with one another in order to do such things as share clients, share facilities, jointly raise money, jointly purchase goods or services, or share staff or other professional consultants (Hasenfeld, 1983; Levine & White, 1961). This form of sharing may be very formal, and it may establish a legal relationship between organizations. In this regard, if cooperation reaches this degree of formality, then political cooperation may be easier to pursue because of the history and experience of working together in a business relationship. In short, political partners may become trading partners and vice versa.

Communitywide coordination can reduce turbulence and uncertainty in the task environment, and organizations should be constantly scanning the task environment to determine the areas where voluntary cooperation is possible, and, in some cases, where this voluntary cooperation may lead to legal and contractual obligations among organizations (Hasenfeld, 1983).

One of the most common areas where interagency cooperation and coordination can occur is through client referrals. Clients or their families call one agency, which then refers them to another agency, and so on. Over time, agencies help each other out by making referrals to each other. These arrangements are usually informal, yet they still solidify the relationships among many organizations. In turn, under some circumstances, agencies who jointly refer clients to each other may want to establish a more formal information and referral system that is automated and may include a central intake telephone number. These kinds of centralized information and referral systems are becoming more popular as the concept of case management is more widely used in the human services (Kane & Kane, 1987). The main difficulty with the centralized information and referral system is that some of the organizations participating in the system may want to select only a small number of the other agencies to give referrals to. When this happens, the idea of a comprehensive pool of agencies loses its viability and a subsystem of agencies develops. Nevertheless, the organizations that participate in joint information and referral systems are prime candidates for additional coalition activity that is more political in nature.

OTHER RESOURCE SHARING

One of the themes so far is that organizations can cooperate in a wide variety of areas to achieve nonpolitical goals, and this cooperation, in turn, has payoffs for the operation of a coalition in which these organizations may be members. There are a few other modes of cooperative interaction worth mentioning briefly that are voluntary, informal, and noncontractual in nature (Holland & Petchers, 1987). These modes of interaction reinforce good interorganizational exchanges and make other forms of coalitional activity more viable.

In terms of clients, it is very helpful for organizations to use informal case conferences around problem clients. The resulting collegiality allows a number of organizations to achieve some sort of professional consensus without the necessity of bringing in a third party or a paid consultant. Informal collaboration also serves to link the organizations to each other more closely, and this makes client referrals between organizations smoother and more effective.

When organizations invite other organizations to certain staff training and staff development sessions, relationships among staff are further strengthened. Even without developing a contract or more formal joint sponsorship of these sessions, it is possible for organizations to invite professionals from other organizations informally to benefit from the training. Reciprocity allows each organization to share the expertise of the people doing the training. In some cases, smaller organizations might not even have the resources for training or staff development unless other organizations are willing to share their resources with them. This, of course, opens the door for collaboration in another area where the resource-poor organization may be better able to reciprocate.

Another area of collaboration is the informal sharing of space and equipment. Again, there may be no formal contractual agreement, but rather helpfulness and reciprocity are the guides. One organization may let another use its meeting room or boardroom, or it may lend an overhead projector or other audiovisual equipment or supplies temporarily. These informal exchanges will make more formal ones easier to develop when the circumstances require more formality.

Finally, there is the whole area of joint sponsorship of special events such as fund-raisers, community forums, conferences, workshops, and legislative days. These events need not necessarily involve any exchange of money. Rather, one organization may have the resources to put on the event, but, to make it successful, they may seek symbolic sponsorship from other organizations in the community. Regardless of who pays for the event, the main point is that much can be gained by joint sponsorship; this type of collaboration can lead to payoffs in other areas as well.

MERGING AGENCIES AND PROGRAMS

Organizations that interact both formally and informally with one another may occasionally find themselves in a position where one organization is failing financially and the programs and services that organization is delivering will have to be terminated unless another organization agrees to absorb them. It may, for example, be the case that an organization is failing because of only one program or service it is responsible for. The organization may not be able to remain solvent despite the success of some of its other programs or services. Under these circumstances, it may be wise for the failing organization to seek a partner in the task environment who is willing to absorb its more successful programs or services. Generally, healthy organizations in the human services do not merge as they might in the private sector in order to create monopolies. Mergers in the human services are more likely to be the result of successful organizations absorbing popular and needed programs or services from organizations that are failing (Turem & Born, 1983). In times of retrenchment, in particular, the frequency of mergers increases. Organizations that are active in coalitions will have a better chance to find willing and suitable organizations to absorb their programs or services in the event that economic circumstances require this type of action. Coalitions bring together organizations with shared interests, and therefore participation in the coalition may have another advantage for organizations experiencing financial setbacks.

SUMMARY

This chapter has stressed a number of broad practice guidelines. First and foremost, it is very helpful if coalitions recognize that their members require a mix of incentives to sustain their interest in a coalition. As a result, coalitions that strive to achieve both political and nonpolitical goals and provide the widest array of incentives for participation will be more viable and the furthest along in terms of institutionalization and permanence. In our experience, broad-based coalitions with a mix of goals are more stable than purely political ones because coalitions that are not used exclusively for political advocacy can fall back on other activities and goals if their memberships become burned out or the coalitions falter in their political agendas. Coalitions with a mix of goals are better able to adapt and sustain themselves over time and move toward permanence.

Second, and by implication, a plan of action that includes both political and nonpolitical goals and a set of mechanisms for periodically assessing where the interests of the members of the coalition are will provide a coalition with a solid framework and set of guidelines for pursuing its interests.

Finally, the leaders of a coalition will find it important to identify clearly the spillover effects of nonpolitical collaboration and cooperation. As illustrated in this chapter, there are many nonpolitical activities that enhance the relationships and harmony among organizations. When concerted political action is necessary, there is a strong foundation for joint action that has been developed over time through these various modes of nonpolitical interorganizational cooperation. While political goals may be paramount to a coalition, successful coalitions also pursue nonpolitical goals as well, and this effort generally will enhance, not diminish, the overall credibility and legitimacy of the coalition in the community.

EXERCISE FOR PRACTITIONERS

A very important exercise for any practitioner is to analyze as thoroughly as possible the task environment of an individual organization for coalition-building purposes. Therefore, take an organization with which you are familiar (or that you currently work in) and first identify in detail the task environment, or the specific set of organizations and groups with which your organization exchanges resources and services on a regular basis. Indicate for each organization in the task environment how frequently your organization has exchanges with that organization. Then identify two or three areas where more sharing might be helpful in the future, especially with those organizations with which exchanges have been infrequent in the past. Next, suggest a few strategies for improving nonpolitical organizational exchanges with these organizations. Evaluate these strategies in light of what a coalition operating in your community may formally adopt as one of its nonpolitical goals for the next year.

Chapter 6

IMPROVING THE UNDERSTANDING OF COALITIONS IN THE HUMAN SERVICES

The key to success of a coalition is having a middle-class and professional membership, a formal organization and staff, good access to decision makers, dramatic issues to work on, clients that are very appealing to the general public and the media, and both tangible and intangible resources available for the coalition to draw upon. (from an interview with a member of a successful coalition)

The above quote aptly captures many of the central points raised in this book. The characteristics of successful coalitions illustrated in this quotation are straightforward and very concise. In order to pursue the question of success still further, participants at a recent national conference who took part in a workshop on coalition building in the human services were asked to identify from their own experiences what characteristics successful coalitions had and, alternatively, what characteristics unsuccessful coalitions had (Alliance for Care, Miami, April 1987). To the surprise of few people attending the workshop, strong coalitions were described as ones that had clear-cut missions or purposes, professional and/or middle- and upper-class members, a narrow set of agenda items that they were attempting to further, adroit leadership, and a deserving client group or cause that they were advocating for. On the other hand, unsuccessful coalitions were described as ones having no compelling mission or purpose beyond information sharing and education, no clear focus or agenda, ill-defined membership, poor leadership, and clients or causes that were difficult to advocate for.

Subsequent discussions in this workshop indicated that there was substantial consensus among the participants about these characteristics. A wide variety of coalitions were illustrated in the discussions. Coalitions advocating for runaway youth, missing children, the handicapped, the mentally ill, the homeless, and the homebound elderly, among others, were exemplified in the group discussion. Besides being representative of a wide diversity of coalitions, participants in the workshop also came from across the United States. This variety makes their observations about what constitutes success even more reliable. In the context of this book, participants in the workshop were able to reflect in action effectively, using their own experiences along with concepts presented in the workshop.

However, what was striking during the discussion was that a predominant agency perspective and bias surfaced almost immediately. Most of the participants were employees of nonprofit agencies, and they indicated in the discussions that their first loyalties were generally to their agencies and not the coalitions they were members of. There was considerable agreement in the workshop that as long as coalitions did not seriously threaten the agendas or the images of their agencies, participation was not frowned upon; in fact, it was encouraged. On the other hand, when conflicts arose between coalitions and their agencies, the participants indicated that they knew where their homes were.

Herein lies a major dilemma facing most coalitions in the human services that have members on the staffs of existing organizations or agencies. The dilemma, as one participant in the workshop suggested, is this:

> Coalitions serve a purpose in our communities, but they are not foremost to us because their purpose is either secondary to our other responsibilities or the coalition just takes up too much of our valuable time. If I have to make a choice, I drop out of the coalition.

Increasingly, the leadership for many coalitions will be likely to come from the staffs of agencies rather than from community leaders or professionals who do not have any agency or organizational affiliations (Brilliant, 1986). It is also very likely that the future of the human services will continue to require the use of coalitions as long as austerity, budget cuts, and prioritization continue to dominate the fiscal environment. As one well-known commentator in the human services argues, uncertainty and scarcity foster the widespread use of coalitions (Weisner, 1983). Therefore, more practitioners with a better knowledge base for understanding coalition dynamics are very much needed in the human services.

IMPROVING KNOWLEDGE FOR PRACTICE

A major premise of this book is that the enhancement of knowledge about coalitions can come from careful observation and analysis of practicing coalitions. This has been referred to as "reflection in action." Using this concept, practitioners learn frequently by reflecting on the phenomenon before them while at the same time reviewing their prior understanding of the behavior involved (Schon, 1983). Thus a practitioner becomes a researcher. A case study can generate a new theory, and the practitioner is not dependent on the categories of established theory and technique. In this way, reflection in action can proceed. Reflective inquiry is a way of developing new knowledge for practice.

The case materials presented in this book are valuable because they identify the major practice guidelines that come from careful reflection by the thoughtful coalition members interviewed. As the cases indicate, there is considerable similarity in the evolution or stages of development of coalitions in the human services, the use of strategies and tactics to achieve both political and nonpolitical goals, and the techniques used for managing coalitions once they have been formed.

The question of the durability of coalitions is of considerable interest to many practitioners as well because thoughtful reflection on how to maintain and further develop a coalition has far more practical use in the human services than trying to theorize, as a lot of the current literature does, about how and why coalitions form. My central argument is that knowledge about coalition development and maintenance may be gained more readily through careful reflection about existing coalitions than through any other research strategy currently available.

It is also probably true that the processes underlying the formation of coalitions are significantly different from the processes used to maintain coalitions successfully (Wright & Goldberg, 1985). In this regard, the human service professions and the academic community are challenged to identify more practice guidelines that can be derived from reflective inquiry about practicing coalitions. Since the 1980s witnessed a significant increase in the use of coalitions, we now need to turn our attention to improving our knowledge base about the dynamics of coalitions, especially the ways in which coalitions move through various stages of development and strive for permanence.

WHY THE DURABILITY
OF COALITIONS IS IMPORTANT

The reality for many coalitions is that the priorities of the membership often change over time, and, as a result, there is a tendency in these coalitions to keep broadening their agendas, to expand their memberships to correspond to the new agendas, and to move toward permanence as they adapt to these new issues and challenges (Black, 1983). It is possible that the responsiveness of a coalition to certain community issues and problems may be lessened when the breadth of the coalition's agenda increases too rapidly. As discussed in Chapter 3, there are forces pulling most coalitions together, that is, trying to make them tighter, more focused, and more specific in purpose. Correspondingly, there are also counterforces in most coalitions that want them to adapt, expand their membership, and continually redefine their purpose. This is inevitable. A major theme that emerges from a reflection on the cases in this book is that coalitions, once formed, tend to persist and move toward permanence.

This inevitable movement toward permanence creates some confusion about the real meaning of the term *coalition*. In the context of this book, it has been stressed that the literature refers to coalitions mainly as temporary alliances formed by actors, agencies, and organizations to achieve a limited set of objectives. Further, coalitions in the earliest stages of development use resources jointly, but these resources are relatively unstable.

Perhaps the most telling characteristic of many coalitions is that members may withdraw at any time and the coalition may disband if too many members drop out. This characterization fits the more traditional meaning of *coalition,* and the bread-and-butter, consciousness-raising, and network coalitions illustrated in Chapter 2 capture the essence of these more temporary alliances. In each case, these types of coalitions can and do succeed, but often they may go out of existence after a period of time.

On the other hand, the cases also illustrate another aspect of coalitions, particularly with preassociations, prefederations, and pre-social movements. What happens with some, but certainly not all, coalitions is that over time they move toward permanence. Gradually, they broaden their missions to include a wide range of objectives, they secure permanent resources, they attempt through recruitment to stabilize and screen their members, they plan their strategies more carefully, they coordinate their tactics more efficiently, and they secure staff to carry out day-to-day activities. Also, they are able to blend more effectively the achievement of both political and nonpolitical goals. In short, they develop over time a more structural order and degree of institutionalization in which each aspect of development described above represents another stage of organizational development (Perlmutter, 1969; Selznick, 1957).

One interpretation of the analysis presented in this book is that when practitioners reflect in action, they will probably conclude that they should buy into more planning, more formalized rules of governance for their coalitions, more coordination of their activities with other groups in the community, and the acquisition of more permanent resources to implement their agendas. What may be lost in this movement toward permanence and further institutionalization are spontaneity, responsiveness, and the ability to tackle emerging and sometimes volatile community issues. The more temporary the alliance, the less shackled it is by time-consuming organizational processes, procedures, and agreements.

Nevertheless, unless a coalition takes on the features of another type of social organization as discussed in Chapter 2, movement toward permanence and a greater degree of institutionalization is not necessarily undesirable. In fact, as seen in some of the cases and the reflections of coalition members, it can result in a greater ability of the coalition to achieve its objectives. As pointed out earlier, if a compelling issue is not dealt with by an existing coalition, another coalition may form to deal with it. In turn, this coalition can provide a safeguard to those who might argue that certain concerns in a community might be ignored by more permanent coalitions.

More durable coalitions represent a new type of coalition that is rarely discussed in the literature. As indicated in Chapter 1, coalitions are mainly portrayed as temporary alliances, but this book has demonstrated that some coalitions can have more permanence and exhibit a greater degree of institutionalization than was previously thought (Boissevain, 1974; Hill, 1973; Kahan & Rapoport, 1984; Wilson, 1973).

The issue of durability should now be clearer: As long as a coalition maintains a balance in its membership, retains the centrality of its political purpose, and does not bargain away control, especially control over resource allocation, to a separate and centralized administrative authority in the community, it will remain as one of the most viable instruments for change in the human services.

Movement toward permanence may be desirable as long as the members of the coalition feel that the benefits of membership still exceed the costs of joining and participating in the coalition. The beauty of a fluid, democratic system, where the use of groups to further political and nonpolitical agendas is encouraged, is that disgruntled or dissatisfied members of a coalition can always start a new coalition, develop a reconstituted or spin-off coalition, or try to have their interests represented through an interest group or a political party.

EXERCISE FOR PRACTITIONERS

A LOCAL COALITION IN ACTION:
A HYPOTHETICAL CASE STUDY

In this final exercise, a hypothetical case is presented that illustrates the dynamics of coalition development. Read the case carefully. At the end of the case are ten questions that probe many of the points discussed throughout the book. First try to answer these questions yourself, and then, in a group discussion, compare your answers with those of other practitioners. You will see by this time that your ability to reflect in action can be improved by using and discussing a case study and integrating previous knowledge with careful reflection about the case. Finally, read the brief answers to the questions presented at the end of the case and compare these answers with your own conclusions and those of the group with which you discussed the case. These brief answers summarize some of the major points and practice guidelines presented in the book.

Background

The state is not only one of the fastest growing states in the Sunbelt, but the continued heavy in-migration of retired people has made the state a showcase for the rest of the country in terms of how an increasingly aging society will evolve. Of particular interest is the fact that while elderly retirees still continue to come to the state in large numbers, many are also returning to their states of origin, especially when physical, mental, and financial problems become unmanageable for them. The statistics show that the state as a whole has gained 350,000 people over the age of 60 during the past five years (in-migration minus out-migration).

The state's elderly population reached 20% of the state's total population in 1990 and is projected to reach 24% by the year 2000. These figures are significantly higher than the national average for other states. The county follows the overall demographic patterns of the state, except that the net population gains are more modest. Specifically, the county has had a net gain of 5,000 people over 60 years of age in the past five years. Analysis by the Area Agency on Aging further reveals that in-migrants are generally younger, healthier, and more economically secure than those leaving the state. However, there is still a significant segment of the population that remains in the county and that is over 80, frail, and at or below the poverty level.

This at-risk group is also disproportionately Hispanic and Black. The picture, then, is one of affluent and healthy elderly coming in, some elderly leaving, and a significant number of elderly already in the county moving into the at-risk category. Estimates are that this at-risk group will increase by 50% each decade through the year 2010. In numerical terms, the county expects to have 10,000 more at-risk elderly by the turn of the century and 20,000 more by 2010. This at-risk category will need help of all kinds, and the county is bracing for an increased demand for services.

The county is both multiethnic and multiracial. As of 1985, 35% of the elderly were Black, 22% were Hispanic, 5% were Jewish, and 38% were nonminority and White. Estimates are that the Black and Hispanic elderly population will continue to grow in numbers while the Jewish and nonminority White elderly population will continue to shrink in numbers. The county has a diverse set of agencies and service providers. The local United Way indicates that there are 105 distinct nonmedical social service agencies serving the elderly in the county. Many of these agencies service specific geographic areas and, as a result, serve well-identified racial or ethnic client groups.

Other agencies have a more mixed clientele. While there are a few large agencies with budgets in the millions of dollars and staffs that are highly professionalized, most of the agencies are small, rely heavily on volunteers, and survive from year to year on small budgets. There is competition among agencies for resources and, in some cases, competition for the same clients. It is quite difficult to get agencies to cooperate on issues of mutual concern since each must protect its turf if it is to survive. Recent program cuts in Washington will exacerbate the problem since many agencies are likely to take two or three successive annual cuts in their budgets. Therefore, survival for many is critical, and most thoughtful observers in the county think that joint agreements, coordination, mergers, and outright agency closings will be more common than ever before because of the fiscal environment. The service providers in the county formed a council a number of years ago to discuss issues of mutual concern. The council now has 60 members who meet regularly to share information and concerns.

Besides the 105 nonmedical agencies serving the elderly, there are nine major community-based hospitals, five active health maintenance organizations (HMOs), a medical school and hospital complex, and two gerontological centers. There is an expressed concern that many elderly are still either underserved or unserved by the existing institutions and agencies. Members of the council fear that the problems and needs of the elderly have become secondary to the agendas and programs of the existing agencies and institutions in the community. Most members agree that there is a real need for this community to develop a capacity to respond to the emerging and critical needs of the elderly.

The Early Days

In 1982 and 1983, the state undertook a major study of the long-term care needs of the elderly. The underlying philosophy of the state was to preserve the autonomy and independence of the older person for as long as possible, and this philosophy was followed by the support and efforts of the state to keep older people in their own homes and out of very costly institutions. As long as the appropriate services could be provided, living at home was almost universally desirable as an alternative to institutionalization. Many of the service providers in the county come into contact with older people who need support of some kind to remain independent.

Nevertheless, there were many at-risk elderly who had no contact with service providers or had contacts that were not helpful. Some elderly sought services from agencies that could not help them directly, and these agencies did not have the time or the ability to refer these people to the appropriate agencies. Many elderly went unserved or were underserved by the existing agencies. A recognition of this problem within the community led to discussions in different forums, among them the Council of Service Providers and a Special Task Force on Long-Term Care organized by the Area Agency on Aging.

Although community awareness was high in 1985, there was no organized and systematic attempt to deal with the problem at that time. In these early days, information sharing and the development of consensus about the problem took place informally and in a very ad hoc way. Still, momentum toward solving the problem seemed to be gaining because of a fortuitous set of circumstances. Because of severe budget constraints and the desire to keep people out of costly institutions, the state was eager to support and encourage community-based programs that would preserve the independence of the elderly.

At the same time, the media and various advocate groups continued to dramatize the plight of elderly people living alone in an alienated urban environment. Stories of people dying at home and being discovered by neighbors, scenes of elderly people not getting out of the house more than a few times a month, and stories focused on lonely and depressed elderly people who were not part of any social support system filled the local newspapers and received attention from TV stations. During this period, the federal government changed its reimbursement system to hospitals by adopting the DRGs, which in turn forced elderly patients to leave hospitals and return home before their illnesses were over. Insurance companies and HMOs were very eager to keep people at home and out of costly hospitals, and they continued to encourage more use of home-based services and less use of in-patient hospital treatment.

These circumstances caused many community leaders to focus on the gaps in the service system that dealt with the at-risk elderly who wanted to remain in their own homes for as long as possible. The county became a prime setting for constructive problem solving.

Building a Presence in the Community

In the summer of 1985, a concrete opportunity presented itself. A major national foundation interested in the problems of aging decided to encourage demonstration programs around the country that would show how a local consortium of community-based agencies could come together and work cooperatively to develop a coordinated and integrated system of services for those frail elderly at risk who chose to remain at home. Some of the members of the Council of Service Providers received notice from the foundation that money would be available for demonstration programs that could put together a consortium approach in their community. This opportunity stimulated a small group of service providers to call an informal meeting of agencies to see if there was any interest in applying for a grant from this foundation.

Initial meetings were of an information-sharing nature. After a few months, a working group of about 30 agencies joined together to submit a grant application to the foundation. The reason for this coming together was apparent. All the agencies felt that if the grant proposal was written in a way that facilitated future cooperation, there might even be a way to improve their own respective services and thus enhance their own missions. Once consensus was reached on the objective of submitting a grant, the information-sharing process became more formal.

Regular meetings were planned, minutes were taken, materials were sent out ahead of time, and a timetable for action was established. Up to this point, participants had given their time sporadically, but once a formal agenda for the group was set, administrative tasks needed to be completed on time. One of the larger agencies in the community donated the time of two professional staff members to the consortium. These people organized the materials, sent out the meeting notices, took the minutes, and, ultimately, wrote the grant proposal.

The consortium of agencies continued to meet throughout 1985. It agreed upon a focus for the group that led to creating a centralized information and referral system. Each consortium member would be able to refer clients it could not serve adequately. The information and referral system, to be called a clearinghouse, would then make a referral to the appropriate agency. It was agreed that if no appropriate agency existed, the coalition would lobby for the development of a new service in the community. What disagreement there was centered around how the clearinghouse would be organized, who would have administrative responsibility for it, and how it would be staffed.

The primary incentive for participation of the agencies in the consortium to this point was that each agency would be able to use a centralized referral system for clients needing more or different kinds of services. The agencies, it was anticipated, would then be more efficient, and, in some cases, they might even get more referrals themselves. Because there was a clear-cut purpose, staff support, and incentives for participation in the consortium, the coalition was quite effective. The proposal was submitted to the foundation, and there was much optimism that this networking approach would serve the community well.

Achieving Desirable Outcomes

The coalition of agencies called itself a consortium only because the foundation limited applications for funding to consortia. While there was a chairperson who ran the meeting during the time that the group was putting the proposal together, the group really had only a donated staff and no formal identity, no officers, no stationery, or any of the other characteristics usually associated with more formal and permanent coalitions. Late in 1985, the foundation informed the group that its proposal would not be funded.

For the next six months there were no meetings, and the agency people who had participated in the consortium never met as a group, even though some of them networked around other issues and concerns. The ad hoc effort had been successful, but now the group had no mission or purpose. The chairperson of the group met socially one Sunday with two other members of the original consortium, and they decided to take a stab at getting the group together again. The original group had a reunion early in 1986, and the results were very interesting.

A consensus existed that the group had enjoyed the process of meeting around the grant, and they were proud of their product (i.e., the proposal). After some discussion, the group decided to meet monthly and to develop a new agenda for action. The chairperson of the original group urged the creation of a professional association of service providers. At a subsequent meeting the association became known as the Coalition for Independence and Autonomy for the Elderly, or CIA for short. Bylaws were drawn up, officers were elected, a formal meeting time and place were established, and modest dues were collected from the members.

At an early meeting, following its formal organization, but after some debate, CIA membership was opened up to some individuals who had no formal agency affiliation. Within three months the membership of CIA went from 25 to 30 agencies, and 25 individual members also joined the group. With 55 people and a budget of $2,000, CIA was in business. Initial meetings focused on getting the coalition organized and formalized. At these sessions information was presented to the membership on budget cuts, sources of alternative funding, legislative changes, and new ideas about organizing home care programs. Attendance at meetings was good and conflict was minimal.

In the spring of 1986, the president of CIA organized a small group to write a $15,000 grant proposal to a local foundation. The proposal was to fund six microcomputers for agencies that wanted to interchange their client files and records. This proposal was funded, and the six agencies developed a mechanism for improved transfer of clients and client information. Although the proposal represented a small amount of money to the six agencies, it demonstrated to the agencies that joint action through the coalition could have immediate payoffs for the members. This early success could be viewed as a more symbolic victory than a tangible one, but it created incentives for continued participation by members. A few weeks later, three members of CIA went to the state capital to lobby for the budget that channeled money to many home care programs in the county. Their efforts were success-ful and they were very pleased when the state not only maintained the current budget level for the home care programs, but also increased that level by 5% for the next fiscal year. Again, immediate results created additional incentives for continued participation by the members.

Finally, in the summer of 1987, the coalition organized a fund-raiser to help generate resources for CIA. The event was attended by 150 people. Prominent social and political leaders attended the cocktail party and auction. The event not only raised money for CIA, but it gave members and their friends and associates an opportunity to interact and network. The opportunity to socialize was an important incentive for many members to continue their affiliation with the coalition. The $5,000 raised by the event was earmarked for mailings, conferences, training, and travel. Practically speaking, the coalition had been able to attract members for a wide variety of reasons, and early tangible successes had helped to set the stage for continued participation.

Establishing Permanence

By the fall of 1986, membership in the coalition had increased to 85. The new members came from an adjacent county. About half of these were agency based and half were independent members with no agency affiliation. The leadership group organized a weekend retreat to develop an agenda for the succeeding year for CIA. The retreat drew 60 members who agreed that seven committees should be established for the next year. These included the following:

(1) Strategy Committee: would guide the overall operations of the coalition and its activities

(2) Talent and Recruitment Committee: would survey the membership and find out time availability and tasks that members would be interested in performing

(3) Long-Range Planning Committee: would compile data on service needs, review the literature on at-risk elderly, and pursue foundation funding

(4) Communications Committee: would organize a phone bank and all special mailings and would develop a newsletter

(5) Special Events/Fund-Raising Committee: would develop plans for receptions, fund-raisers, and annual board meetings

(6) Media and Public Relations Committee: would develop press releases and stories for media

(7) Monitoring and Oversight of Legislation Committee: would follow all legislative and administrative changes affecting member agencies

More important, the retreat established a clear-cut set of objectives for the coalition for the next year. After much debate, five objectives were established:

(1) to develop brochures, handouts, and materials on CIA, to be circulated throughout the community, stressing the fact that the coalition was focusing on the frail elderly regardless of income status

(2) to encourage the state to set aside a proportion of its training dollars for paraprofessionals working in home care agencies of all kinds

(3) to approach the county United Way for funding for social welfare agencies (not just home care agencies) that wanted to computerize their client records and referral mechanisms and to suggest that funding should come through a competitive bidding process open to all social welfare agencies in the county

(4) to approach a foundation to fund a detailed study of the needs for home care among the elderly in the county

(5) to strengthen all aspects of coordination between member agencies so that clients will be served better

As 1988 began, CIA had a clear-cut mission and an operating organizational structure to implement its plan. While the full list of objectives did not appeal to all of the members, most members found at least one agenda item of interest to them. As the coalition began to implement its strategy for 1988, two troublesome issues surfaced. First, even though the coalition had 85 members, the president usually turned to three particular members for advice on how to run the coalition. Some members resented this behind-the-scenes approach, and at one meeting they openly challenged the organizational management. The president argued persuasively that he would share power in the future, but he needed a way to access member opinions and attitudes on a regular basis. A special meeting was set aside for discussion of proposals to remedy this situation.

Second, as the agenda for action became more clear-cut, members were increasingly asked to lobby actively for the objectives of the coalition. Contacts had to be made with state legislators, local county commissioners, United Way board members, and representatives of other funding sources. Some members were uncomfortable with this type of aggressive political marketing of the CIA agenda. Others felt just as strongly that without this aggressive marketing, there would be no reason for the coalition's existence, since it would be unable to actualize its goals. Debate centered on "professional behavior" and what constituted appropriate behavior on the part of the members. The final meeting of 1988 was indeed controversial. One of the members designated by CIA to lobby in the state capital for more training dollars for home care workers had sent a letter to all the members of the coalition, urging them to contribute to Representative Tom Riley's reelection campaign. At the meeting, one member said:

> It is time to draw the line about what this coalition is all about. If I become a partisan, I will lose my self-respect, the confidence of my board, and the respect of my staff. After all, we are professionals and we need to remember that.

QUESTIONS

Answer these questions first by yourself and then in a group discussion:

(1) What kinds of factors lead to the formation of coalitions among agencies and organizations?

(2) What are the major elements of a successful coalition?

(3) What are the different types and forms of coalitions?

(4) How can you keep a coalition going when it experiences a setback?

(5) Can coalitions become too political? Are there consequences to the politicization of members?

(6) What are some of the lessons to be learned from the case presented above? (Think of a lesson as something that emerges from a positive experience that is worth repeating by another coalition.)

(7) Which is more desirable, an ad hoc coalition that accomplishes its objective and then goes out of existence or a coalition that becomes permanent but must increasingly manage internal conflict?

(8) What types of incentives cause people to join coalitions?

(9) When should an agency or individual withdraw from a coalition?

(10) How aggressive should coalitions be? What image should they project to others in the community?

PARTIAL ANSWERS

(1) What kinds of factors lead to the formation of coalitions among agencies and organizations?

Many factors lead to the formation of coalitions. The most common is a dramatic issue or crisis that forces the community to react (e.g., budget cuts, a newspaper story about an abused person, a shutoff of electricity, malnutrition). How the issue gets on the agenda is less important than how the agencies or organizations react to it. Often, the government, the United Way, or a foundation may issue a call for service coordination or cooperation and either mandate or encourage coalitions that will attempt to achieve this type of cooperation. A charismatic leader may organize a coalition to serve his or her own personal or ideological needs, independent of a crisis or dramatic event. Finally, a coalition may be an outgrowth of other interactions that take place among agencies or other organizations. A new coalition can emerge because agencies and organizations regroup around another, more focused issue. Thus some agencies and organizations go one way while others go another. Here the process is one of regrouping, not necessarily of coming together for the first time.

(2) What are the major elements of a successful coalition?

There seems to be considerable consensus that a successful coalition has the following elements: a clear-cut purpose or mission, a combination of political and nonpolitical goals, a plan of action, an organizational structure and a method of governance that emphasizes periodic feedback from the members, stable leadership, clear-cut incentives for participation by the members, frequent and ongoing successes, an effective internal communication network, and leaders within the coalition who take a developmental perspective on the coalition and think about the various stages of organizational development that must be followed in order to move the coalition toward institutionalization and permanence.

(3) What are the different types and forms of coalitions?

We usually think of ad hoc coalitions as groups that form around a single issue and then disband when the issue is resolved or people lose interest in it. These are referred to as bread-and-butter, consciousness-raising, and network coalitions. More permanent coalitions that have some longevity as well as the ability to accommodate other issues over time are referred to as preassociations, prefederations, and pre-social movements. However, the critical difference is that these more permanent groups survive, endure, and almost always move beyond a single issue or purpose. These more permanent coalitions then take on features of more formalized organizations. They are very likely to have elected leaders, bylaws, stable sources of funds, stable memberships, formal agendas, and so on.

(4) How can you keep a coalition going when it experiences a setback?

The key is to focus on an issue that can be resolved successfully so that the membership will see that the group can work together effectively. Sometimes a series of less important issues need to be resolved before more difficult and controversial issues can be tackled. Pragmatic successes must be achieved periodically to keep the incentives for membership involvement high. In this context, nonpolitical goals may be easier to achieve and success at achieving these goals may create a bond and enough trust for the group to tackle more difficult political goals at a later time.

(5) Can coalitions become too political? Are there consequences to the politicization of the members?

There are always trade-offs when more political involvement by the membership is required. It is not easy to draw the line and there is often no clear answer about where that line should be drawn. However, the key point is that coalitions should discuss the issue openly and not avoid it. Usually, an open process will produce an organizational position on what the degree of politicization of its members should be. Politicization of membership is of particular concern to coalitions that include both agency heads and professionals.

(6) What are some of the lessons to be learned from the case presented above? (Think of a lesson as something that emerges from a positive experience that is worth repeating by a coalition.)

Consider the following practice guidelines as lessons:

- Capitalize on external events or crises whenever possible.
- Always be aware of the incentives of the members for involvement so that activities are planned to maximize participation.
- Strive for organizational clarity and clarity of mission.
- Devote considerable time to developing an effective communication network within the coalition.
- Try to achieve successful outcomes periodically to keep membership interested.
- Develop internal decision-making processes that will keep coalition members coming together even if only for symbolic purposes.
- Set up a strategy committee to develop a plan of action and monitor the day-to-day activities of the coalition.
- Find a role for everyone and avoid elitism in organizational governance.
- Diagnose and network with key actors in the public policy environment on a regular basis.
- Periodically review the plan of the coalition—especially the strategies, the approach, the style of presentation, and the tactics—and make sure the elements are consistent with one another and supported by the membership of the coalition.

(7) Which is more desirable, an ad hoc coalition that accomplishes its objective and then goes out of existence or a coalition that becomes permanent but must increasingly manage internal conflict and, many would argue, also becomes more conservative in terms of an orientation toward social change?

There is no one right answer here. There are pros and cons concerning both kinds of coalitions. Ad hoc coalitions can be immensely successful, but they are a drain on resources because the start-up costs are considerable each time a new coalition has to be formed. While a permanent coalition does not have to reinvent the wheel, it will constantly have to deal with issues that require much discussion and debate. A changing agenda always produces some conflict.

(8) What types of incentives cause people to join coalitions?

There are many, and none of them should be overlooked in the management of the coalition. The principal incentives for participation in coalitions are as follows:

- ideological or symbolic benefits
- tangible benefits for the member's agency or organization
- tangible benefits for the individual (i.e., job or contacts)
- social benefits for the individual
- enhancement of the agency's reputation/image
- improvement of client situation
- civic duty
- distribution of critical/updated information on the field of service to members

(9) When should an agency or individual withdraw from a coalition?

An agency or individual should withdraw when the negative benefits of membership outweigh the positive ones. Time spent at coalition functions is time subtracted from agency time and personal time. Each participant will balance his or her schedule somewhat differently. Usually, coalition time is low in priority, and this is to be expected. The point here is that coalitions should be very careful not to waste members' time.

(10) How aggressive should coalitions be? What image should they project to others in the community?

Professional or agency-based coalitions will have to draw the line, but generally direct political involvement such as candidate endorsement, giving money to candidates or parties, and formally involving partisans in coalition activities is frowned upon in these coalitions. Community-based coalitions on balance are more supportive of direct political involvement. However, each coalition should discuss this issue and establish a position. Community-based coalitions have more flexibility and usually can be as political as they choose without experiencing negative consequences.

SUGGESTIONS FOR THE
FUTURE STUDY OF COALITIONS

There are some additional questions about the maintenance and development of coalitions that should be explored in more depth in the future in order to add to our current knowledge base. First, leadership in coalitions is one of the areas where we need better knowledge for practice (Brilliant, 1986). For example, it is not clear from these case studies whether a single charismatic leader is critical to the development of a coalition or whether a collegial group of highly motivated people can be just as effective. In addition, the importance of leadership, regardless of the type, and its impact on organizational maintenance and development needs to be looked at. Uncertainty in coalitions provides the opportunity for persuasion, manipulation, and even deception on the part of leadership.

Since coalition members often show uncertainty in their participation and because coalition membership is voluntary, leadership can be crucial to overcoming these barriers to involvement. It would also be helpful to identify the critical tasks for leadership. In retrospect, these cases illustrate that starting the coalition, defining its mission and modifying it when necessary, managing conflict, developing the issue agenda, and being responsible for the quality control connected to implementing political strategy and tactics are at the heart of what effective leadership should be responsible for. The question of what other kinds of tasks are essential for leadership to perform should be investigated.

Second is the issue of how much conflict in a coalition can be tolerated before it becomes destructive to the achievement of the coalition's major goals. Conflict, especially around purpose and mission, can be healthy in any group or organization, but the critical question is how much divergence in preferences can be handled and constructively managed by the leadership. Since coalitions are primarily vehicles for achieving common objectives, the degree of conflict that can be handled should be looked at carefully.

Third, and closely connected to the level of tolerable conflict, is the question of the type of membership base a coalition should strive for. One might argue for mixed-base membership—that is, agencies, professionals, and community residents. However, regardless of members' agreement with the ends of a coalition, mixed membership may lead to differences about the means to be used to achieve these ends. This was illustrated in the case studies in terms of professional neutrality, agency commitment and loyalty, and partisan affiliation. More investigation of the appropriate mixes of membership is needed. For example, one hypothesis is that it is representativeness of the coalition, not its size, that often dictates its legitimacy and ultimate success.

Fourth, much more needs to be known about why coalition members decide to join and then later leave coalitions. There are many personal and organizational dilemmas raised by coalition membership and particularly the political activity required on the part of the members. This type of information is needed by coalition leaders as they plan their strategies. Since coalitions are voluntary and have a temporary quality to them, more information about membership motivation and behavior would be useful. A start may be to focus on those members who drop out of coalitions. This would identify the factors that make the durability of coalitions difficult.

Fifth and finally, coalition organizers must concern themselves with how coalitions can become more structured without losing their ability to respond to changing and emerging issues. Balancing organizational survival with organizational responsiveness is not always easy, but the techniques that can be used to do this can lead to permanence without sacrificing substance.

IMPLICATIONS FOR PRACTITIONERS

I began this book with the assertion that coalitions are viable instruments for practitioners to use in their communities to achieve common goals that affect their clients in the human services. I argued further that leadership in the human services needs and would benefit from practitioners who know both the art and the science of coalition building. In a broader context, I also suggested that additional political advocacy skills among human service professionals are needed and that more emphasis on these skills is especially important because of the current fiscal environment in the human services.

At a more personal level, coalition involvement on the part of human service professionals is very valuable for direct practitioners who may be confined to working with clients and their families and who have few outlets for their frustration about some of the policies and programs they are frequently asked to implement. Coalitions allow these types of professionals to have an impact on a broader set of issues. Coalitions also allow practitioners who have neither the time nor the patience to join political parties, interest groups, or more formal organizations to participate in groups that have narrow and focused purposes. Coalitions make it possible for such practitioners to avoid the social trappings of many larger and more formal organizations. Direct practitioners are very much needed in coalitions. Because they have close contact and involvement with clients, they can make special contributions to the setting of coalition agendas. Some of the most persuasive arguments that coalitions can make to decision makers often come from people who know the problems firsthand, rather than from people who know the problems secondhand as a result of reading reports, attending meetings, and doing research. Finally, there is a normal tendency for most formal organizations (such as agencies) to resist coalition formation except on an ad hoc basis (Wilson, 1973). The tendency to protect their own agencies or organizational domains makes it difficult for people in communities to tackle many cross-cutting problems that go beyond a single agency or program. Only when enlightened human services professionals are willing to look beyond their jobs, their agencies, and their professions by following their instincts and joining coalitions will many of the really tough issues of contemporary society be addressed adequately.

APPENDIX: QUESTIONNAIRE

The following questions were asked in all the interviews completed with members of 13 practicing coalitions. A total of 25 interviews were completed with either members or the leaders of these coalitions. The interviews were tape-recorded because the questions were open-ended. The direct quotes used throughout this book come from these tape-recorded answers to our questions.

(1) Please start by telling us briefly about your coalition. When was it formed? Why was it formed? What is its main purpose? Who were the key people who got things started? What fiscal and other resources does the coalition use? How did you acquire these resources?

(2) Now describe the membership of your coalition for us. We are particularly interested in how this membership has changed over time. How many members do you have? Can you describe them or give us a profile? What have been their motivations for participating in your coalition? Have they changed? Are there any factions? How are members selected or recruited into the coalition? Have there been any major changes in the membership since the inception of the coalition? Please describe any major changes in some detail.

(3) Tell us a little about what resources the coalition has available to it. Financial? Nonfinancial? Who do you compete for resources with? Generally describe the environment that the coalition competes for resources in.

(4) We are interested in the day-to-day practices of the coalition. How often do you meet? What types of communication patterns exist? Is there a newsletter? Other types of correspondence between members? How is

the coalition managed on a day-to-day basis? Are there any staff? Are they paid? Does the coalition use a telephone bank? Are there any other devices used by the coalition to facilitate communication?

(5) Now tell us about your basic approach or strategy within the coalition. Has it worked? Could you illustrate some of the more successful tactics? Are there tactics that have not worked well? Has your basic approach or strategy changed over the years? Explain.

(6) How does the coalition present its case to the community or decision makers? What image do they seek to project? Do they present their case emotionally? Politically? As experts or technicians? Or some combination?

(7) Please describe specifically the key people in your coalition. What roles do they play? Why are they leaders in the coalition? What makes them influential with the other members?

(8) Identify any problems that have troubled the coalition since its beginning. How were these problems resolved? Do they remain unresolved? (Probe for problems like factionalism, inadequate resources, lack of clear focus, poor leadership, poor communication, poor day-to-day management, and the use of inappropriate strategies and tactics.)

(9) Please describe the coalition's major accomplishments and outcomes to date. Be very specific.

(10) In your judgment, what kind of factors would jeopardize the future of the coalition?

REFERENCES

Abrams, H., & Goldstein, S. (1982). A state chapter's comprehensive political program. In M. Mahaffey & J. Hanks (Eds.), *Practical politics: Social work and political responsibility.* Silver Spring, MD: National Association of Social Workers.

Adrian, C., & Press, A. (1968). Decision costs in coalition formation. *American Political Science Review, 62,* 556-563.

Alexander, C. (1982). Professional social workers and political responsibility. In M. Mahaffey & J. Hanks (Eds.), *Practical politics: Social work and political responsibility.* Silver Spring, MD: National Association of Social Workers.

Bacharach, S., & Lawler, E. (1980). *Power and politics in organizations: The social psychology of conflict, coalitions, and bargaining.* San Francisco: Jossey-Bass.

Bell, W., & Bell, B. (1982). Monitoring the bureaucracy. In M. Mahaffey & J. Hanks (Eds.), *Practical politics: Social work and political responsibility.* Silver Spring, MD: National Association of Social Workers.

Black, T. (1983). Coalition building: Some suggestions. *Child Welfare, 62*(3), 263-268.

Boissevain, J. (1974). *Friends of friends: Networks, manipulators, and coalitions.* New York: St. Martin's.

Brager, G. (1968). Advocacy and political behavior. *Social Work, 13,* 5-16.

Brilliant, E. (1986). Social work leadership: A missing ingredient? *Social Work, 31,* 325-331.

Bryson, J. (1988). *Strategic planning for public and nonprofit organizations.* San Francisco: Jossey-Bass.

Burghardt, S. (1987). Community based social action. In A. Minahan (Ed.), *Encyclopedia of social work* (18th ed., Vol. 1). Silver Spring, MD: National Association of Social Workers.

Burns, J. (1978). *Leadership.* New York: Harper & Row.

Carter, R. (1983). *The accountable agency.* Beverly Hills, CA: Sage.

Checkoway, B. (1987). Political strategy for social planning. In F. Cox (Ed.), *Strategies of community organization* (4th ed.). Itasca, IL: F. E. Peacock.

Cox, F. (Ed.). (1987). *Strategies of community organization* (4th ed.). Itasca, IL: F. E. Peacock.

Cyert, R. (1975). *Managing the non-profit organization.* Lexington, MA: D. C. Heath.

Dean, W. (1977). Back to activism. *Social Work, 22,* 369-373.

133

Dear, R., & Patti, R. (1981). Legislative advocacy: Seven effective tactics. *Social Work, 26,* 289-296.

Dempsey, D. (1982). Establishing ELAN in a state chapter. In M. Mahaffey & J. Hanks (Eds.), *Practical politics: Social work and political responsibility.* Silver Spring, MD: National Association of Social Workers.

Dexter, L. (1969). *How organizations are represented in Washington.* Indianapolis: Bobbs-Merrill.

Dluhy, M. (1981a). *Changing the system: Political advocacy for disadvantaged groups.* Beverly Hills, CA: Sage.

Dluhy, M. (1981b). *Social change: Accessing and influencing the policy development process at the state and local levels.* Washington, DC: U.S. Department of Health and Human Services, Youth Development Bureau.

Dluhy, M. (1984). Moving from professionalism to political advocacy in the human services: How to organize a successful statewide political effort in youth services. *Journal of Sociology and Social Welfare, 11*(3), 654-683.

Dluhy, M. (1986). Developing coalitions in the face of power: Lessons from the human services. In B. Checkoway (Ed.), *Strategic perspectives on planning practice.* Lexington, MA: D. C. Heath.

Dluhy, M. (1987). Homelessness as a public concern: How to develop a community approach to solving the problem. In F. Cox (Ed.), *Strategies of community organization* (4th ed.). Itasca, IL: F. E. Peacock.

Dluhy, M., et al. (1988). *Approaches to linking policy and research in aging.* Jerusalem: JDC-Brookdale Institute of Gerontology.

Downs, A. (1967). *Inside bureaucracy.* Boston: Little, Brown.

Edelman, M. (1971). *Politics as symbolic action.* Chicago: Markham.

Fairlie, H. (1988). Talking about my generation: Whatever happened to a dignified old age. *New Republic, 198*(13), 19-22.

Fallows, J. (1982). Entitlements. *Atlantic Monthly, 250*(5), 51-59.

Friesen, B. (1987). Administration: Interpersonal aspects. In A. Minahan (Ed.), *Encyclopedia of social work* (18th ed., Vol. 1). Silver Spring, MD: National Association of Social Workers.

Gamson, W. (1968). Coalition formation. In D. Sills (Ed.), *International encyclopedia of the social sciences.* New York: Macmillan.

Garner, L. (1989). *Leadership in human services.* San Francisco: Jossey-Bass.

Gilbert, N., & Specht, H. (1974). *Dimensions of social welfare policy.* Englewood Cliffs, NJ: Prentice-Hall.

Haggstrom, W. (1987). The tactics of organization building. In F. Cox (Ed.), *Strategies of community organization* (4th ed.). Itasca, IL: F. E. Peacock.

Hasenfeld, Y. (1983). *Human service organizations.* Englewood Cliffs, NJ: Prentice-Hall.

Hasenfeld, Y. (1987). Program development. In F. Cox (Ed.), *Strategies of community organization* (4th ed.). Itasca, IL: F. E. Peacock.

Haynes, K., & Michelson, J. (1986). *Affecting change: Social workers in the political arena.* New York: Longman.

Heclo, H. (1979). Issue networks and the executive establishment. In A. King (Ed.), *The new American political system.* Washington, DC: American Enterprise Institute.

Hill, P. (1973). *A theory of political coalitions in simple and policy making situations.* Beverly Hills, CA: Sage.

Hinckley, B. (1979). Twenty one variables beyond the size of winning coalitions. *Journal of Politics, 41,* 192-212.

Holland, T., & Petchers, M. (1987). Organizations: Context for social service delivery. In A. Minahan (Ed.), *Encyclopedia of social work* (18th ed., Vol. 1). Silver Spring, MD: National Association of Social Workers.

Howe, E. (1978). Legislative outcomes in human services. *Social Services Review, 54,* 173-188.

Humphreys, N. (1979). Competing for revenue sharing funds: A coalition approach. *Social Work, 24,* 14-18.

Jecker, N. (1987). *Excluding the elderly: A reply to Callahan.* College Park: University of Maryland, Center for Philosophy and Public Policy.

Kahan, J., & Rapoport, A. (1984). *Theories of coalition formation.* Hillsdale, NJ: Lawrence Erlbaum.

Kane, R., & Kane, R. (1987). *Long term care: Principles, programs, and policies.* New York: Springer.

Katz, R. (1988). Skills of an effective administrator. *Harvard Business Review* [Special issue], pp. 45-57.

Keefe, W., & Ogul, M. (1977). *The American legislative process* (4th ed.). Englewood Cliffs, NJ: Prentice-Hall.

Kingston, E., Hirshorn, M., & Cornman, M. (1986). *Ties that bind: The interdependence of generations.* Washington, DC: Seven Locks.

Kravitz, D., & Iwaniszek, J. (1984). Number of coalitions and resources as sources of power in coalition bargaining. *Journal of Personality and Social Psychology, 47*(3), 534-548.

Lauffer, A. (1983). *Grantsmanship* (2nd ed.). Beverly Hills, CA: Sage.

Levine, S., & White, R. E. (1961). Exchanges as a conceptual framework for the study of interorganizational relationships. *Administrative Science Quarterly, 5*(4), 583-601.

Lindblom, C. (1965). *The intelligence of democracy.* New York: Free Press.

Lyden, F., & Miller, E. (1982). *Public budgeting* (4th ed.). Englewood Cliffs, NJ: Prentice-Hall.

Lynch, T. (1979). *Public budgeting in America.* Englewood Cliffs, NJ: Prentice-Hall.

Marin, P. (1987). Helping and hating the homeless. *Harper's Magazine, 274*(1640), 39-49.

Mathews, G. (1982). Social workers and political influence. *Social Services Review, 58,* 617-628.

Matthews, D. (1960). *U.S. senators and their world.* Chapel Hill: University of North Carolina Press.

Murnighan, J. (1978). Models of coalition behavior: Game theoretic, social psychological and political perspectives. *Psychological Bulletin, 85,* 1130-1163.

Nelson, B. (1984). *Making an issue of child abuse: Political agenda setting for social problems.* Chicago: University of Chicago Press.

Oleszek, W. (1978). *Congressional procedures and the policy process.* Washington, DC: Congressional Quarterly Press.

Olson, M. (1968). *The logic of collective action: Public goods and the theory of groups.* New York: Schocken.

Ornstein, N., & Elder, S. (1978). *Interest groups, lobbying and policymaking.* Washington, DC: Congressional Quarterly Press.

Patti, R. (1983). *Social welfare administration: Managing programs in a developing context.* Englewood Cliffs, NJ: Prentice-Hall.

Perlmutter, F. D. (1969). A theoretical model of social agency development. *Social Casework, 50*(8), 467-473.

Pierce, D. (1984). *Policy for the social work practitioner.* New York: Longman.

Rein, M. (1976). *Social science and public policy.* New York: Penguin.

Riker, W. (1962). *The theory of political coalitions.* New Haven, CT: Yale University Press.

Roberts, M. (1984). *Building a political organization to support a coalition's policy position.* Unpublished manuscript, San Diego State University, School of Social Work.

Robert Wood Johnson Foundation. (1985). *Request for proposal for unified information and referral systems.*

Salamon, L., & Abramson, A. (1985). *The new budget and the nonprofit sector.* Washington, DC: Urban Institute.

Sarri, R. (1987). Administration in social welfare. In A. Minahan (Ed.), *Encyclopedia of social work* (18th ed., Vol. 1). Silver Spring, MD: National Association of Social Workers.

Schon, D. (1983). *The reflective practitioner: How professionals think in action.* New York: Basic Books.

Seidman, H. (1970). *Politics, position, and power.* New York: Oxford University Press.

Selznick, P. (1957). *Leadership in administration.* New York: Harper & Row.

Sharwell, G. (1982). How to testify before a legislative committee. In M. Mahaffey & J. Hanks (Eds.), *Practical politics: Social work and political responsibility.* Silver Spring, MD: National Association of Social Workers.

Siegel, L., et al. (1987). Need identification and program planning in the community context. In F. Cox (Ed.), *Strategies of community organization* (4th ed.). Itasca, IL: F. E. Peacock.

Siporin, M. (1987). Resource development and service provision. In A. Minahan (Ed.), *Encyclopedia of social work* (18th ed., Vol. 1). Silver Spring, MD: National Association of Social Workers.

Smith, V. (1979). How interest groups influence legislators. *Social Work, 24,* 235-239.

Staples, L. (1987). Can't ya hear me knocking: An organizing model. In F. Cox (Ed.), *Strategies of community organization* (4th ed.). Itasca, IL: F. E. Peacock.

Stevenson, W., et al. (1984). *The concept of coalition in organization theory and research.* Unpublished manuscript, University of California, Irvine, Graduate School of Management.

Stewart, R. (1981). Watershed days: How will social work respond to the conservative revolution? *Social Work, 26,* 271-273.

Thursz, D. (1971, January). The arsenal of social action strategies: Options for social workers. *Social Work,* pp. 27-34.

Tropman, J. (1987). Policy analysis: Methods and techniques. In A. Minahan (Ed.), *Encyclopedia of social work* (18th ed., Vol. 2). Silver Spring, MD: National Association of Social Workers.

Turem, J., & Born, C. (1983, May-June). Doing more with less. *Social Work,* pp. 206-210.

Villers Foundation. (1987). *On the other side of Easy Street: Facts about the economics of old age.* Washington, DC: Author.

Walzer, M. (1973, Winter). Political action: The problem of dirty hands. *Philosophy and Public Affairs, 2,* 160-180.

Warren, R. (1977). *Social change and human purpose.* Chicago: Rand McNally.

Weiner, H. (1984). Coalition building: The Pennsylvania experience. *Community Mental Health Journal, 20*(2), 159-162.

Weisner, S. (1983). Fighting back: A critical analysis of coalition building in the human services. *Social Services Review, 57*(2), 291-306.

Whitaker, W. (1982). Organizing social action coalitions: WIC comes to Wyoming. In M. Mahaffey & J. Hanks (Eds.), *Practical politics: Social work and political responsibility*. Silver Spring, MD: National Association of Social Workers.

Wildavsky, A. (1988). *The new politics of the budgetary process*. Glenview, IL: Scott, Foresman.

Wilson, J. (1973). *Political organizations*. New York: Basic Books.

Wolk, J. (1981). Are social workers politically active? *Social Work, 26*, 283-288.

Wright, J., & Goldberg, A. (1985). Risk and uncertainty as factors in the durability of political coalitions. *American Political Science Review, 79*(3), 704-718.

ABOUT THE AUTHORS

Milan J. Dluhy is currently Professor of Social Work and Public Administration at Florida International University in Miami. He has also served as Acting Dean of the School of Public Affairs and as Associate Director of the Southeast Florida Center on Aging at FIU. Prior to his present position, he held faculty positions at the University of Michigan and American University. His career has also included working as a Senior Policy Analyst with the U.S. Department of Health, Education and Welfare and serving as a consultant to the states of Florida, Michigan, and Vermont, and to many local governments and numerous coalitions and advocacy groups. He has authored or coauthored five books as well as many other professional publications in the areas of social welfare policy; programs and policies for youth, the elderly, and the homeless; housing; and political advocacy.

Sanford L. Kravitz is currently Distinguished Professor of Public Affairs at Florida International University in Miami. He has had a 40-year career in social work at the local, state, and federal levels. He served as Associate Director of the Community Action Program in the Office of Economic Opportunity. He has been an Associate Professor of Social Planning at the Heller School, Brandeis University, and was the founding Dean of the School of Social Work at the State University of New York at Stony Brook, a position he held for 10 years. He has worked extensively with a wide variety of community groups and organizations during his multifaceted career, and continues to maintain a high level of involvement with community-wide and statewide social planning and advocacy groups.